Contents

Expanded Table of Contents

11 Writing a Feature Article: Structure 151

12 Writing a Feature Article: Outlining, Drafting, Revising 171

13 Writing a Feature Article: Style 185

14 Final Steps to Publication   205

15 Business, Legal, and Ethical Practices for Writers   215

Index   233

Writing Feature Articles

1

Magazine Writing Today

WHAT YOU WILL LEARN IN THIS CHAPTER

• Magazines are published on almost every topic imaginable, and they provide many opportunities for freelance writers.

• The Internet has afforded new opportunities for feature writers.

• Freelance writers must be good writers and good marketers of their work.

• Magazines serve three main purposes: to inform, entertain, and inspire.

• Writers can better equip themselves to write for magazines by analyzing their content and editorial policy.

Good Housekeeping and *Sports Illustrated*
Ceramics Monthly and *Civil War Times*
Salon.com website and *Southern Living* on an e-reader

Magazines come in all shapes and sizes. The examples above show the proliferation of high-circulation consumer magazines, specialty or "niche" magazines, and online magazines. While the magazine industry is changing in appearance and sensibilities, it is still alive and kicking. And there are countless opportunities for freelance writers to find a place for their work.

This book covers the opportunities and practices for writing feature articles and getting published in newspapers, consumer and trade magazines, and online publications. This chapter will focus primarily on feature writing for general, consumer magazines — but many of the principles apply to feature writing for other types of publications also.

Just a few years ago, some people were heralding the end of magazines as a viable media outlet. Magazines, these experts said, would go out like the dinosaurs — replaced by online-only publications, e-readers, and other digital devices and innovations. People, they said, would no longer want to flip through a print magazine.

It's nice to know that soothsayers aren't always right. Print magazines look as if they are here to stay. In fact, there are thousands in print. *Writer's Market* (an annual guide that lists magazines that accept freelance material from writers) includes 8,000, although many magazines aren't even featured in the guide. In a typical year, there are between 700 and 1,000 start-ups of new magazines, according to Samir Husni, a professor at the University of Mississippi and a leading expert on the magazine industry.

Magazines are available at newsstands and in grocery stores. They are read in doctors' offices. They are ordered through subscription and still delivered in mailboxes. They cover a wide variety of topics and reach out to a multitude of audiences. *Writer's Market* lists more than 40 different categories of consumer magazines and more than 50 different categories of trade magazines.

Traditional publishing will continue to be a powerful force in the future, and the number of magazines may even increase, according to Joe Pulizzi. He is the founder of the Content Marketing Institute and author of books on publishing and advertising. "In the era of iPads and apps," he says, "there is most definitely a role for print. Print still excites readers."

Albert Read, general manager of Conde Naste publications, says that "magazines are efficient and allow depth, which is a need that readers still have today."

While it's evident that print magazines are still viable and popular with the public, it is important to realize that the times are indeed changing. Magazines are evolving, and the way readers get their information from those magazines is also evolving. Readers now often visit a magazine's website for additional information. They may use an App (application) to subscribe digitally to a magazine. They may read their magazine via a Kindle, Nook, or other e-reading device. They may visit online-only magazines via the Internet.

It is important to realize that the market for writing is wide-open. It involves both traditional magazines and Internet-based publications.

"Our writing does have to change somewhat," says freelance writer and journalism professor George Daniels. "It tends to be shorter now, and we have to market ourselves cross-platform between mediums.

"But I actually think there is going to be a new novelty in printed publications. Seeing your name in print and on paper is different and still exciting. I think it's more of a both-and situation, instead of an either-or one."

It seems, then, that magazines in the coming years will operate in two ways … in print and in technological advancements.

Writers for magazines must, then, be prepared to write for the changing industry. They must know how to find markets for their articles, how to submit query letters by email and regular mail, how to work with editors, how to revise their work, and how to write salable articles — whether for a print edition or an online version.

In changing times, though, it's important to remember that some things stay the same.

Good writing is good writing.

The things that have always made a magazine article good are the same things in operation today. "Good" is an elusive term, but we seem to understand it when we read an article that affects us in a positive way. The attributes of good writing — quality information, interesting sources and quotes, a lively writing style, characterization, dialogue, setting, description, and thematic quality — will always be important. As a writer, you must strive always to write the best article possible — whether that article will be read in a traditional paper publication or online.

Good marketing is good marketing.

The best feature writers — especially freelancers — are those who can make themselves viable and relevant. They "sell" themselves to editors and publications by coming up with good ideas and then marketing the ideas in practical, professional, and creative ways. Writing a good query letter for regular mail or email is still of upmost importance. Forging relationships with editors — through correspondence, face-to-face meetings, and online contact — is still vital in being published on a regular basis.

And those things never change.

Magazines Today

Look around your home or office. Chances are your eyes will alight on a magazine of some shape or fashion within mere moments.

There are tens of thousands of magazines. They are published in New York

City and Chicago, but also in Charleston and Corpus Christi. They have circulations of 2 million, but also circulations of 20,000. They are geared toward women, men, pet owners, hikers, teenagers, children, walkers, and car collectors ... in fact, almost any group you can think of.

Writer's Market — an invaluable resource for freelance writers that lists thousands of magazines and book markets, as well as literary agents — includes the following categories of consumer magazines:

Animal	Humor
Art & Architecture	Inflight
Associations	Juvenile
Astrology, Metaphysical, and New Age	Literary and Little
Automotive and Motorcycle	Men's
Aviation	Military
Business and Finance	Music
Career, College, and Alumni	Mystery
Child Care and Parental Guidance	Nature, Conservation, and Ecology
Comic Books	Personal Computers
Consumer Service and Business Opportunity	Photography
	Politics and World Affairs
Contemporary Culture	Psychology and Self-Improvement
Disabilities	Regional
Entertainment	Religious
Ethnic and Minority	Retirement
Food and Drink	Rural
Games and Puzzles	Science
Gay and Lesbian Interest	Science Fiction, Fantasy, and Horror
General Interest	Sex
Health and Fitness	Sports
History	Teen and Young Adult
Hobby and Craft	Travel, Camping, and Trailer
Home and Garden	Women's

Writer's Market also lists various categories of trade magazines ranging from Advertising to Marketing and PR to Veterinary (with things like Church Administration, Law, and Real Estate in between).

If you're interested in writing for magazines, all of this information is good news. Thousands of magazines are published, both in print and online — and all of them need feature articles to fill their pages.

Anatomy of a Magazine

Open any of the types of magazines listed above, and look at the pages. You'll find that they have some common characteristics. It's important for you, as a prospective writer, to examine those pages and learn as much as you can about the magazines you want to write for. Pay particular attention to the following items:

Cover

A magazine's cover is the first glimpse you have of what the magazine is really all about. It provides art (usually a photograph related to one of the features inside), blurbs about the features inside, and practical information such as the name of the magazine and the issue price.

Table of Contents

As you learn to study magazines in order to become a better prepared writer, you will learn the value of analyzing the table of contents. You will find the different columns or departments the magazine has, the number of feature-length articles in an issue, and the topics of all of the articles.

Editor's Letter

If you want to determine what some of the editor's particular interests — or pet peeves — are, the editor's letter is a great place to gain insight into his or her personality and interests. The letter usually is located a page or two after the table of contents. It will usually mention articles in that particular issue. It will give you some insight into the types of topics that the editor is particularly drawn to.

You might even develop ideas for articles based on the table of contents and the editor's letter, by seeing what topics the magazine regularly features.

Columns and Departments

Magazines usually have shorter articles that appear in the front or in the back of the magazine as columns or departments. These features — usually written by regular writers of the magazines — are important to every issue. They are normally one page in length or shorter, but sometimes there may be three or four smaller boxed articles on one page. The departments are on specialized topics. A women's magazine, for example, might have a Makeup or Advice department.

Feature Articles

Feature articles make up the meat of a magazine's editorial content and fill in what is called the *editorial well* of the magazine. The "well" consists of the center pages, often uninterrupted by advertising. It is where all the quality content resides. The articles that make up the well are longer, normally at least two to four pages, and sometimes longer than that. They usually have accompanying artwork such as photographs, illustrations, or other graphics.

Sidebars

Magazines often have sidebars accompanying a feature article. These sidebars — usually graphically boxed in — provide supplementary material. The information usually isn't connected tightly enough to the article to be part of the body of the article, but it supplements the article's topic. Sidebars typically include such things as resource lists, quotes from people, statistics, questions, quizzes, recommended readings, and related tips or advice. For example, an article on helping a teenager navigate a first romantic relationship might include sidebars of famous quotes about young love, definitions of different types of love, and examples of Facebook statuses from teenagers about love.

Pull and Drop Quotes

A popular graphic element found within many articles is a pull or drop quote — a quote pulled from the article that gives a good thematic overview of what the article is about. It's printed in larger type and makes the page visually more appealing. It gives readers insight into the article's main theme or points.

Photographs and Illustrations

The style of a magazine will determine what photographs and/or illustrations it uses. Obviously, a high circulation or big budget commercial magazine will have more financial resources for high quality photographs. Magazines that are more serious in nature may use illustrations more often than photographs. Some magazines will also use graphic elements such as charts and bars to complement the editorial copy.

Photographs and illustrations are an important part of a magazine. They help create the appearance and personality of a publication, and especially good ones can effectively supplement the editorial quality.

Most large magazines have photographers on staff or rely on specific freelance photographers. Smaller, regional, or niche magazines usually don't. They may ask you to provide photographs. If they don't, suggest photos to the editor.

Advertisements

Although feature writers are most interested in the editorial side of a magazine, they also pay attention to its advertisements — for that's where they often best gauge its audience and priorities.

A magazine that advertises high-end fragrances and automobiles reveals an audience on the high-end of the monetary and educational demographic scale. One that advertises exercise equipment and bottled water reveals an audience interested in fitness and health. By analyzing a magazine's ads — and not just breezing by them, or totally ignoring them — you will better understand for whom you are writing.

Why Magazines Are Important

Why do magazines exist? What purpose do they serve?

An un-scientific survey of some people who love to read magazines (but who are not writers) revealed the following reasons why magazines appeal to them:

- "I like to read about people like me. People who have some of the same problems and struggles and roles as I do."
- "My favorite magazine is filled with pretty things. I love to escape through the pages of the magazine, and it shows me places I'd love to go some day and wonderful-looking recipes."
- "Magazines give me information I need on a daily basis. I really like it when I learn something I didn't know before."
- "I'm a sports fanatic. So my favorite magazines fulfill that 'fix' I need for sports information and minutiae."
- "I love to read inspiring stories."
- "Sometimes I don't even read every word of the articles. I just like to have something fun to read."

If you ask yourself why you read magazines, you might come up with similar reasons — or entirely different ones. Thinking, though, about why you read magazines will ultimately make you a better magazine writer.

Magazines generally serve three purposes — to inform, entertain, and inspire.

To Inform

If you think about why you read magazines, the first reason you'd come up

Christina Boufis
"Writing for Women's Magazines"

Q: How did you get into writing for magazines?

BOUFIS: I really fell into writing for magazines. I had just finished my PhD in Victorian literature and women's studies but knew I didn't want to go into academia: I wanted to write. And, after so long in graduate school, I wanted to get out into the "real world."

I started teaching women prisoners at the San Francisco County jail, and, by necessity, since it was so exhausting yet rewarding, I started to write about it. My first article was a feature in *Glamour Magazine*, which I pitched over the phone to the editor. I mistakenly thought all freelance writing worked that way: you called up the editor, pitched her an idea, she said yes, and that was it. It took me years afterwards to realize writing was a business.

Q: Why do you enjoy writing for women's magazines? And what do you enjoy about being a freelance writer?

BOUFIS: I love writing for women's magazines, as I write (hopefully) the kind of articles that I would like to read — ones filled with usable information that can improve my life and health. I also love being a freelance writer because I get to indulge my curiosity, to research a topic that I'm interested in, and to figure out how to present it it in an interesting way. I think it was William Zinsser who said that all writing is a problem to be solved, and every day I get to solve problems. There's great satisfaction in nailing a lead or finding just the right quote or source to bring the topic to life. What's also a boon is that in some ways, I feel as if I'm living my dissertation, which was about women, specifically the construction of female adolescence in the 19th century.

Q: What is different about writing for women than for other audiences?

---

with would probably be, "I want to learn about something." Most magazines, then, are informational first. They provide useful information on many topics for a wide range of different audiences.

Most magazines are filled to the brim with informational and how-to articles — stories that provide information to the reader on a specific topic. They might teach you all the ins and outs of the latest diet, or teach you how to bake a cake, or inform you about all you need to know about Florence, Italy. They provide you with information you might otherwise not receive.

BOUFIS: I'm not sure that the writing is that different — I still have to condense information and present it in a lively and readable format — it's just that I feel closer to the audience. I think of my mother or sister or friends or myself when I write, and I ask myself: What would they (we) like to know? What is most important to our lives? Or what woman or girl is most inspiring and therefore a good candidate to profile for a woman's magazine?

Q: What tips would you give someone who is interested in writing for women?

BOUFIS: First, read the magazines and websites that you love, and absorb the language, the tone, the content of the publication or site. Then ask yourself what's missing. What would you like to see this particular site or publication cover? What inspiring stories of women do you know? Who is doing something interesting in your neighborhood? I've had a lot of success taking a local story — a local woman or girl doing something amazing — and pitching it to national publications.

Q: What are some tips you'd give to people who are trying to break into freelance writing for the first time?

BOUFIS: Be fearless. I knew nothing about how freelance writing worked when I broke in. I didn't know you shouldn't pick up the phone and call editors. I once called an articles editor, and her outgoing message said something like, "Don't send us a manuscript or query. We don't work with freelance writers. Don't leave a message." You know what? I left a message pitching an essay, giving her the title and a one-sentence summary. She called back within 30 seconds and told me to send it. That's how I broke into one of the major woman's magazines.

And, oh, don't let rejection derail you. It is just part of the freelancing life.

Christina Boufis has been published in most of today's popular magazines for women, including *Glamour*, *Natural Health*, Salon.com, and *O, the Oprah Magazine*. She also blogs for www.womansday.com.

As you think about your role and future as a feature writer for magazines, realize the importance of this informational purpose.

To Entertain

Magazines are not read solely for the information they provide. People also read them for entertainment. Readers like to sit down for a few moments (or an hour or two) and find an escape from their normal routine. They like to be entertained — amused, pampered, diverted — by the stories in a magazine.

Magazines can entertain in various ways. They can tell entertaining stories, introduce readers to entertaining people, transport readers to entertaining places. Think about how magazines entertain you; then you can realize how you can write articles that entertain readers.

To Inspire

A third important purpose that magazines can serve is one of inspiring its readers. Readers don't want just to be informed or entertained; they often want to be inspired in some way. They want to be moved by a story they read.

Inspiration can come in many forms. It can come through an article about an individual whose life or story encourages or inspires, about a place that inspires reflection and beauty, about a topic that the reader feels strongly about. In these and in many other ways, a magazine can inspire readers to make their lives better — to feel empowered in ways they may not have felt before reading its pages.

How will you, as a writer for magazines, use your words to inform, entertain, or inspire — or to accomplish all three?

When you understand a magazine's purpose, you can then sense the types of article ideas you can develop, the types of articles you want to write, the style of writing you want to develop, and a sense of purpose as you reach out effectively to readers.

The Magazine Writer

The proliferation and popularity of magazines present many opportunities for writers. With thousands of magazines in existence, logic indicates that there must be plenty of writing opportunities. Magazines need editorial copy — and editorial copy needs writers.

As a feature writer, you will have various opportunities to write for magazines. You might work on staff as a writer or an editor. You might work as a contributing writer for a magazine — that is, not as a regular staff member but as a contributor who writes on a regular basis. You might work as a freelance writer who gets assignments from a number of different magazines. You might work as a freelance writer who drums up assignments of your own by working primarily on speculation. As you can see, there are numerous ways to write for magazines.

Chapter 6 in this book will provide more detailed information about these different types of writers, as well as information about what the life of a freelance magazine writer is like.

Writing for traditional magazines and online publications can be one of the most fulfilling roles you can have. It affords you the opportunity to share your insights and expertise, to reach countless readers, and to hone your writing in a practical and productive way.

Freelance writer Sara Kosmyna says that the opportunities for a feature writer are both endless and exciting, and she can't imagine doing anything else. "Just think of all the subjects out there! From babies to cars, gardening and sewing, to travel and wine. The topics are endless. Whatever your passion, you can become an expert just by writing about what you know and love," Kosmyna says. "And freelancing gives me the opportunity to compose my ideas, to say them clearly on the page, and to have a voice."

Exercises

Each chapter in this book concludes with exercises to help you become a published feature writer. Buy a notebook for your personal writing. Or if you prefer to write on your computer, start a journal file or folder that you can add to as you go along. Do the chapter exercises in this book, in your notebook, or on your computer.

1. Look at the list of types of magazines included in the *Writer's Market* guidebook. Which types of magazines jump out at you? Make a list of them, and consider why you would like to write for these magazines.

2. Why do you like to read magazines? Write a brief (200-300 word) essay stating your reasons.

3. Select one of your favorite magazines and consider how it meets each of its purposes. Write a 250-word essay explaining how it informs, entertains, and inspires you.

4. You need to study magazines — get to know them inside and out — in order to be the best magazine writer you can be. Select one of your favorite magazines (or the same one you used for Exercise 3) and analyze each part of it. Using the checklist below, write a brief description and impressions of each part of the magazine.

Magazine Analysis

Name of Magazine: _____

1. Cover

2. Table of Contents

3. Editor's Letter

4. Columns and Departments

5. Feature Articles

6. Sidebars

7. Pull and Drop Quotes

8. Photographs and Illustrations

9. Advertisements

Writing Features for Newspapers

WHAT YOU WILL LEARN IN THIS CHAPTER

• Newspapers offer a variety of opportunities for feature writers.

• Newspaper feature articles appeal to readers through proximity, timeliness, and often a human interest angle on an otherwise "newsy" topic.

• Newspaper feature articles frequently include the 5 W's, have short leads, are short in length, and must be timely.

*N*ewspapers provide many opportunities for feature writers. While the quality of writing and the general style and format of writing are similar to what one finds in magazines, differences do exist in style and format and even differences in marketing.

Approximately 13,000 print newspapers are published today. Although the number of print newspapers has declined for several years, online versions of newspapers have increased. Most of them — both daily and weekly newspapers as well as online newspapers — accept freelance feature material.

Although newspapers focus mainly on news, most also publish feature material, and even the newsy items are not all hard news. They have a lot of space to fill, and they don't fill it solely with articles on crime and politics. They also publish stories about interesting people, events, and other topics.

Open your local daily or weekly newspaper, and you'll find articles on local festivals and celebrities, travel destinations, and unique happenings. While most newspapers have reporters to cover the important straight news in their reading area, they don't all have enough writers to provide human interest features about their community. Many will, therefore, buy feature articles from local writers.

Elements of Newspaper Feature Articles

What types of articles other than news can freelancers write for newspapers?

Newspapers, to a greater extent than most magazines, prefer stories that have the following characteristics:

• *Proximity*

Readers generally pick up a newspaper to find out what's going on in their local area. Freelance feature articles thus need to focus on a local person, place, event, or issue. This local slant is important to keep in mind as you propose a story. Of course, a few newspapers — such as the *New York Times* or *Wall Street Journal* — reach a national audience. For them, the "local" slant is not as important.

• *Timeliness*

Newspapers are also distinctive because they provide information about current events. Most magazines, which are planned months ahead of time, print articles on topics that are less timely, and their time schedule is usually monthly. Daily newspapers deal with events almost as they happen, and weeklies mainly publish stories about events less than seven days old. Keep these time frames in mind as you're writing. You need to accentuate the timeliness of your topic.

• *Human Interest*

The simplest way to think of a human-interest story is that it focuses on a person. People like to read about other people, and human-interest stories meet that need. Many magazines also publish human-interest articles, but they also publish how-to and other types of articles that are not about people. Newspapers also publish how-to and other articles that are not human-interest ones. Such articles, though, are not as numerous as in magazines, and they usually come from staff members and syndicated columnists. So the best opportunity for freelancers to write for newspapers is with human-interest features (stories about interesting people and what they do).

Understanding these three elements — proximity, timeliness, and human

Writing Feature Articles

The Professional Guide to Publishing
in Magazines, Newspapers, and Online

Cheryl S. Wray

VISION V PRESS

The Author

Cheryl Sloan Wray is a freelance writer, popular writing instructor, and expert on feature writing. She has published more than 1,500 articles in a variety of magazines, newspapers, trade papers, and online publications including *American Profile*, *Home Life*, FamilyFun.com, *The Birmingham News*, *The Upper Room*, *Atlanta Parent*, *Christian Retailing*, and many more. She is the author of *Writing for Magazines: A Beginner's Guide* (a Writer's Digest Book of the Month selection), *Masterpieces of Reporting*, *Great Editorials*, and three other books. She speaks often at writing conferences across the country and has taught magazine writing at the University of Alabama (Tuscaloosa) and the University of Alabama at Birmingham. She can be found online at www.writingwithcheryl.word press.com.

Writing Feature Articles

Copyright 2013 by Vision Press

Vision Press
4195 Waldort Drive
P.O. Box 1106
Northport, AL 35476

Printed in the United States of America

interest — helps freelancers think of article ideas to propose to newspapers. The ideas that can evolve from these elements include such topics as the following:

Sports
Local special events
Food
Travel
Animals/pets
Style
Religion
Opinion
Local celebrities who are well known in their own area of expertise
Local people who have done something interesting, unique, or otherwise newsworthy
A human-interest slant on a news happening

Structure and Style of Newspaper Feature Articles

In writing feature articles for a newspaper, you must use a particular method of writing. You can't simply write as if you were freelancing for a magazine. Some important differences exist between magazine and newspaper features, and you must employ the proper practices in your writing.

The most notable differences between newspaper and magazine writing include the following:

1. Newspaper features include the who, what, when, where, and why of a story.

These details are commonly called the 5 W's. While magazine articles will include all of these aspects, newspaper articles put a stronger focus on them and feature them as close to the beginning of the article as possible. In straight newspaper articles, all five are almost always mentioned in the lead paragraph. In newspaper feature articles, you don't have to adhere slavishly to that principle, but you still need to include the 5 W's near the beginning of the story.

2. Newspaper features have shorter leads.

You may take several paragraphs to develop the lead in a magazine article. In a newspaper article, though, you want to write a shorter lead — usually just the first paragraph or two.

3. Newspaper features are shorter.

You may write 2,000-word articles regularly for magazines, but newspaper features are usually shorter. You will probably be working in the 500 to 1,000-word range.

4. Newspaper features must be timely.

Since newspapers emphasize what has occurred recently, you will probably be writing about something that happened within the last week. Be sure to keep up-to-date on happenings and make the recent nature of your topic an important part of your story.

Even though newspaper features adhere to some specific writing practices, they still can be interesting, compelling, and creative. Topics about travel, people, seasonal events, and the arts allow for more creativity than hard news stories do. You can use many of the same creative, stylistic elements that you would use in magazine stories — such as description, quotes, storytelling, and literary devices. Don't let the newspaper medium scare you into thinking that the writing must be mechanical or boring. In fact, it should not be.

How To Break into Newspaper Feature Writing

Feature writers have several ways available to break into writing for newspapers. The most successful ones are the following:

1. If you live near a small paper, put together a portfolio of sample work, go by the office, and introduce yourself to the editor or feature editor. Let the person know you will work on assignment and also ask if he will take article queries.

2. If you live in a larger market, do the same thing by mail or email. Introduce yourself and your writing, and see what opportunities might be available.

3. Another means of getting published in newspapers is column writing. Can you develop a regular column for your local newspaper on a topic on which you are an expert or have experience? For example, if you are a devotional writer, propose a devotional column. If you travel extensively, propose a travel column. If you're a teacher, propose a column dealing with education issues. Sometimes writers can break into column writing by first submitting letters to the editor and occasional guest essays. Many newspapers are open to such submissions.

4. Another option in writing for newspapers is setting up in business as a syndicated columnist. Syndication involves writing a column that is printed in

numerous newspapers across the state or country. Think of the "Dear Abby" advice column or Dave Barry's humor column. It is not easy to become a syndicated columnist, but syndication is an option that is ideal for feature writers who have a specific specialization. Your expertise may be finance, or travel, or single parenting, or any other topic that appeals to a large audience. Various syndication services — such as Tribune Media Services, United Features Syndicate, and King Features Syndicate — offer opportunities for freelancers. Syndication services are listed in the *Writer's Market* guide. If you want to write columns without going through a syndication service, you may simply email your column to more than one newspaper at a time.

The key to getting started as a newspaper freelancer is to find out what the newspapers need and then present yourself as a good option for helping them meet those needs.

Exercises

1. Obtain a copy of your local newspaper and read the articles in its front news section. What writing characteristics do you see in the articles?

2. Read the articles in the human-interest sections of your local newspaper. Those sections will focus on such topics as travel, lifestyle, business, sports, and outdoor activities. Analyze three of the feature articles. For each one, describe the following three elements:

a. Timeliness

b. Proximity

c. Human-interest in a news event or a local, timely topic

3. Read three newspaper articles and three magazine articles. List five differences you see between newspaper articles and magazine articles.

a.

b.

c.

d.

e.

4. Develop a list of 10 article ideas you could pitch to your local newspaper editor.

a.

b.

c.

d.

e.

f.

g.

h.

i.

j.

Writing for Online Publications

WHAT YOU WILL LEARN IN THIS CHAPTER

• Online publications are the fastest growing publications in the world and provide many opportunities for writing in the future.

• Writing for online markets is different from writing for magazines and newspapers. Online writing is shorter, more succinct, more visual, extremely timely, and more expansive in scope.

The publishing world is changing rapidly — primarily because of the transformation the Internet has created. Millions of websites provide information to readers on a timely basis, and prognosticators believe the Internet will become an even more important part of the publishing business than it is today. As magazines provide their editorial content through websites and online versions, writing opportunities are becoming more and more readily available.

Online Versions of Traditional Magazines

Almost all traditional, print magazines have an online presence. Their digital versions come in either of two basic iterations: as an online version of the print edition or as a separate online entity with information independent of the print edition. Choose any magazine you read on a regular basis and look for it online. It's almost certain to have an online presence.

Consider, as an example, regional parenting magazines. Nearly all of them have online versions of their print publication. Many include online copies of the articles that they print in their paper editions. They then archive the articles so that readers can get access to back issues. The online version often has updated calendars of events, links to relevant advertisers, and blogs by parenting experts.

This sort of online presence is typical of smaller, regional, or niche magazines. They include information from their print versions and some supplementary information unique to their digital version.

Other online versions of print magazines provide a much larger amount of additional editorial content that the magazines have not already printed in their paper editions.

Examples of such publications include entertainment and sports magazines. The regular morning reading of many people's online news, for example, includes stops at such sites as the Internet versions of *Entertainment Weekly* magazine and *Sports Illustrated* magazine. Both of those magazines' online versions (at www.ew.com and www.si.com) provide hundreds of articles that the magazines don't publish in their print versions. Readers can get hourly news on movies, television, celebrities, sports figures, sports events, and commentary.

Online versions of magazines often refer to their sister, print versions — by including an excerpt of a featured print article or advertising the new print issue about to be released — but they have editorial content that is entirely independent of the print versions. The two magazine forms — traditional and online — work in tandem together.

Most print newspapers also have an online home. You can quickly access them through such Internet sites as www.thepaperboy.com and www.50states .com. On Paperboy, for example, you can read newspapers from around the world and from individual American states. The link to Texas newspapers, for instance, provides access to 147 newspapers, ranging from large ones such as the *Dallas Morning News* to small ones such as the *Gilmer Mirror*. Links are available for all states.

Exclusively Online Publications

The Internet has created a space for tens of thousands of online publications. They can be found on literally every topic imaginable. To get an idea of the number of online publications, take the list of categories found in *Writer's Market* and multiply the number 10 times. These publications don't have a print counterpart but are successful in their own way.

You can find online magazines on food, religion, politics, lifestyle, travel, news ... anything that warrants editorial treatment. As a feature writer, you can simply search for a particular topic, and a world of opportunities opens up for you.

As these online publications continue to grow in number, so do the writing opportunities. Some of the ways writers can use online publications include the following:

1. Writing for online versions of print magazines for which they may already write

As freelancers contact, query, and contract to write for traditional print magazines, they should consider the option of writing for the online versions also. Ask the editors about specific opportunities or guidelines for doing so.

2. Writing for online versions of print newspapers

Work with editors of online versions of newspapers in the same manner as you would with an online version of a print magazine.

3. Writing for exclusively online magazines

The methods for writing for online magazines are similar to writing for print magazines. Once you come up with an idea, you must query the editor and try to sell her on the validity of your idea. (Chapter 9 in this book will discuss querying.)

Similarities and Differences

Many of the concepts pertinent to traditional writing, marketing, and publishing are the same ones in online writing, marketing, and publishing. You still have to come up with a good idea, sell an editor on your idea, and provide a quality, finished product.

Some notable differences exist, though, between writing for traditional media and writing for online media. They include the following:

1. Online writing is shorter and doesn't cover as broad a subject area.

Whereas readers of print magazines may spend 10 or 15 minutes with an article that is several pages in length, online readers generally prefer to spend less time with an article. Online articles therefore must be shorter in length, perhaps, for example, 800 words instead of 1,800. With online articles, writers thus must quickly get to the heart of the topic. They have to decide what the most important aspect is and how it can be written about in an effective yet brief way.

Susan Johnston
"Writing for Online Publications"

Q: How did you get started writing for the Web? Did you come to online writing from more "traditional" writing?

JOHNSTON: I've written for both traditional markets and online markets, but I started both around the same time. I found that Web markets seemed more receptive to less established writers, because some veteran writers are magazine purists and because online markets have a constant need for fresh material.

Q: How is Web writing different from magazine writing?

JOHNSTON: Web writing tends to be conversational and sometimes casual. Usually, it's broken into short paragraphs with subheads or bullet points so it's easily digestible on a smart-phone or computer screen. Also, Web articles can be more immediate and timely, while it can take six months or longer for a magazine to go to press.

Q: What advice would you give to writers interested in writing for the Internet?

JOHNSTON: Rates vary widely, but don't feel that you have to write for free. If you do a little digging, you'll find plenty of markets that pay writers. (In fact, I found over 50 for my ebook.) As you gain more experience, you can work your way up the pay ladder.

Also, it's important to understand the difference between online journalism and con-

---

2. Online writing is visual, which means reading online is a visual experience.

Websites have clicks to links, image galleries one can scroll through, and other graphic elements. Freelancers must keep those elements in mind when writing online feature articles.

3. Online writing is extremely timely.

An active and popular website may update its pages every 30 minutes. Articles may appear on the front page for only a day. The changing nature of websites requires that online articles be timely and up-to-date. Online editions of print magazines, on the other hand, will keep articles up longer, "archiving" the contents of the magazines for the entirety of the month and then for some time beyond that.

tent mills. Online journalism is a collaborative process between you and an editor, and it's not the kind of writing you can dash off in 15 minutes off the top of your head. Online journalism may require you to work in keywords and other SEO techniques, but often content mills are targeted entirely at search engines rather than real people, and it comes through in the writing. That kind of writing is typically awkward and stuffed full of keywords.

Q: How do you market yourself as a Web-based writer? For example, with magazines, one writes query letters to editors. Is there a similar or different tactic with Web writing?

JOHNSTON: As with magazine editors, Web editors often assign based on queries. Because there's such a need for content, though, they'll sometimes assign you topics once they know and trust you. That happens with magazine writing, too, but with magazines there's more competition for less real estate.

Q: What else might beginners need to know about Web writing?

JOHNSTON: It requires many of the same skills that newspaper and magazine journalists need: interviewing and reporting skills, an eye for typos and style issues, a constant flow of story ideas, and a love of writing. On top of that, it helps if you can do basic photo editing, add links and keywords, and turn things around quickly yet accurately.

Susan Johnston writes regularly for online sites, with credits at such locations as CitySearch.com, DailyCandy.com, MediaBistro.com, WritersWeekly.com, Yahoo!HotJobs, and Experience.com. She is the author of *The Urban Muse Guide to Online Writing Markets* and can be found online at susan-johnston.com.

---

4. Online writing vastly expands your audience.

   Readers for an article published in an online magazine or website are literally limitless in number because articles are accessible anywhere on the planet.

   Freelancer Terry Wilhite, who often writes for online publications, believes online publishing offers many opportunities to writers. As the publishing world becomes more digital, it's important for the feature writer to consider online publishing in order to have success. He says he's amazed by the readership that his writing can reach, that his audience can be so large. "Building an international audience is not impossible," he says, "but very common. Think about the audience your writing can attain."

Exercises

1. Check out the online versions of traditional print magazines. Some good examples that have a large audience include SportsIllustrated.com, People.com, and SouthernLiving.com. Make a list of items or characteristics that stand out to you.

2. Select three topics — such as women, travel, and cooking — that especially interest you, and then use a search engine to find online publications that relate to those topics. Make a list of 10 potential markets for your writing.

    a.

    b.

    c.

    d.

    e.

    f.

    g.

    h.

    i.

    j.

3. Make a list of 10 ideas for articles you can pitch to online publications.

    a.

    b.

    c.

    d.

    e.

    f.

    g.

    h.

    i.

    j.

4

Writing for Trade Publications

WHAT YOU WILL LEARN IN THIS CHAPTER

• Trade magazines — magazines that focus on a specific industry — provide feature writers with publication opportunities.

• Trade magazines differ from consumer magazines in that they publish articles about specific industries, focus on practical information, and work more with writers through assignments.

• The best ways to market to trade magazines are to keep up-to-date on industry news, find writing opportunities online, locate industry experts, and write letters of introduction to editors.

When you think of magazines, which titles come quickly to mind? Chances are, most people think first of magazines like *Good Housekeeping*, *Sports Illustrated*, *Cosmopolitan*, *Time*, and *People*. Those are all popular magazines that consumers buy at the bookstore, read in the grocery store line, or get in the mail through a subscription.

They don't usually think of magazines with the titles *Boutique Design*, *Egg Industry*, *Machinery Lubrication*, *Vending Times*, and *Restaurant Business*.

Like that first group of *consumer* magazines, magazines in the second group number in the thousands. These *trade* magazines — magazines geared to specific industries — provide an important service to readers across the globe.

Also like consumer magazines, trade magazines take freelance material, and thus they provide numerous opportunities for feature writers.

Writer's Market — an annual guide listing magazines that accept articles from freelance writers — actually lists more categories of trade magazines (56) than consumer magazines (48). Following are the trade categories. As you read through the list, notice the broad range of specific areas.

Advertising, Marketing, and PR
Art, Design, and Collectibles
Auto and Truck
Aviation and Space
Beauty and Salon
Beverages and Bottling
Book and Bookstore
Brick, Glass, and Ceramics
Building Interiors
Business Management
Church Administration and Ministry
Clothing
Construction and Contracting
Drugs, Healthcare, and Medical Products
Education and Counseling
Electronics and Communication
Energy and Utility
Engineering and Technology
Entertainment and the Arts
Farming
Finance
Fishing
Florists, Nurseries, and Landscapers
Government and Public Service
Groceries and Food Products
Home Furnishings and Household Goods
Hospitals, Nursing, and Nursing Homes
Hotels, Motels, Clubs, Resorts, and Restaurants
Industrial Operations
Information Systems
Insurance
Jewelry
Journalism and Writing
Law
Lumber
Machinery and Metal
Maintenance and Safety
Management and Supervision
Marine and Maritime Industries
Medical
Music
Office Environment and Equipment
Paper
Pets
Plumbing, Heating, Air Conditioning, and Refrigeration
Printing
Professional Photography
Real Estate
Resources and Waste Reduction
Selling and Merchandising
Sport Trade
Stone, Quarry, and Mining
Toy, Novelty, and Hobby
Transportation
Travel
Veterinary

Most beginning feature writers may be unaware of trade magazines. With so many of them, though, they offer attractive opportunities. Even though popular consumer magazines may seem more glamorous, writing for trade magazines can be lucrative, for they usually pay more than the average consumer magazine.

Consumer Magazines vs. Trade Magazines

While trade magazines offer many opportunities for freelancers, they are different from consumer magazines in important ways. Some of the differences include the following:

Trade magazines publish articles on specialized industries.

Because trade magazines are service-oriented toward specific industries, their articles tend to be specialized. They usually emphasize practical information and are technical in nature, and they require that writers understand the ins-and-outs of a particular industry. Consumer magazines, on the other hand, publish articles on more general topics and don't require as much specialized knowledge.

Trade magazine editors assign a large percentage of articles.

Trade magazines depend more on an editorial calendar than most consumer magazines do. Most issues need technical articles on specific topics. Thus, editors tend to assign many articles to writers. Because so many articles are planned, editors accept fewer pitched ideas. Freelance writers have better luck submitting queries to consumer magazines. With experience, though, they can get opportunities to work on assignment with trade magazines.

Trade magazines don't emphasize writing creativity.

The trade magazine market does not offer much room for writing creativity, simply because most articles are intended to be informative and service-oriented. Writers should always be on the lookout, though, for article ideas that can give a touch of human-interest to a trade magazine. Most editors appreciate such ideas.

Finding Trade Writing Opportunities

Your first question, as you begin pondering the possibility of writing for trade magazines, probably goes something like this: "I'm not an expert on a particular industry. I don't know about retail business, or manufacturing, or trucking. How can I write for magazines that focus on such areas?"

While trade magazines do want knowledgeable writers, as an experienced feature writer you actually have an advantage. *You have writing expertise.* Many contributors to trade magazines are experts but not writers. They know about their area of specialization, but they don't necessarily know how to write well about it. Even though, at the beginning, you may know little about the specialization, you can become knowledgeable enough. By interviewing and getting information from industry experts, you become an expert by proxy. Combine that knowledge with writing talent, and you can publish in trade magazines.

As you consider writing for trade publications, you simply need to learn how to find the markets. Here are some of the best ways to do so:

Utilize the latest Writer's Market.

Writer's Market provides pages and pages of information on trade magazines, and you can use it as you do in looking at opportunities in consumer magazines. Identify magazines for which you want to write because of a personal interest or because you know how you can find experts in the specific subject area. Read the publications' writer guidelines and pay close attention to magazines that use "work-for-hire." That description means the editor assigns stories to freelancers without the writer having to pitch story ideas. You can simply convince the editor ahead of time that you are a qualified writer with published credits and that you would be an asset to the magazine.

Locate trade publications online.

A great resource for learning about the trade magazine industry is the website www.TradePub.com. There you will find hundreds of publications listed in dozens of categories, from "agriculture" to "utility and energy." You can look at online copies of the publications, link to the publications' websites, and learn more about the industry in general. Also remember to locate the online presence of print magazines. Most trade magazines have website versions, often with information that complements the print versions. You can find specific information on writing opportunities, as well as information on how to contact editors.

Keep up-to-date on industry news.

The more you know about specific industries, the better equipped you will be to write for their magazines. Get on as many industry e-mail lists as you can, especially if there are local chapters of trade industry groups in your area. Attend local meetings, get to know people in the industry, and let them know that you are a writer who'd like to work with experts on potential articles.

Locate experts.

This approach may seem a little backward to the process — but, instead of finding experts after you come up with an article idea, consider instead first finding an expert source. The source then can be the foundation of an article. For example, you might read in your local newspaper a story about a horticulturalist who has received a national award for research on vegetable mildew. That expertise could provide the basis for an article for a magazine dealing with the nursery industry. Use the contacts you obtain through the industry websites, emails, and local chapters to develop possible articles for magazines.

Write Letters of Introduction to editors.

While feature writers may certainly send query letters to trade magazine editors, many editors actually prefer what is called an LOI or "letter of introduction." Email a letter to an editor, introducing yourself as a published feature writer who is interested in writing for the magazine. Mention your published articles, your particular industry interests, and any specific industry contacts you have. In effect, you are applying for a job as a freelance writer on assignment. You may get an immediate response or assignment, or the editor will tell you that she will keep your information on file. Keep a record of the editors who respond to you and follow-up with them at a later date.

Sending LOIs can help you get a steady roster of clients for your writing business while you continue to send queries to editors at consumer publications.

Characteristics of Effective Trade Magazine Articles

Effective articles for trade magazine have distinctive characteristics. They include the following:

1. Articles provide practical, useful information.

All magazines have a strong "how to" presence, and this characteristic is as true with trade as consumer magazines. Whereas consumer magazine readers primarily want to know how to make their personal life better, trade readers want to know how to perform better in their specific industry.

2. They utilize quality research.

Trade magazines want articles with meaningful, helpful information. To provide such information, you need to do quality research. Use the best sources and experts you can find. Talk to industry leaders and workers. Go online and gather background information on the topic. Even though you may not be an expert with experience in the industry, you need to come across as a professional

Deborah Lockridge
"Writing for Trade Magazines"

Q: How did you get into work with trade publications?

LOCKRIDGE: Like most journalism students, I did not graduate from college with the intent of going into trade, or B2B (business-to-business) journalism. It's a shame more don't, because there are lots of opportunity in this field. My first job was working for a small publisher of a magazine for farmers featuring organic growing, specialty crops and direct marketing. I then moved on to a company that published magazines for the trucking and construction fields. Today I work for a company that specializes in the trucking industry.

Q: What is the difference between consumer and trade magazines, particularly the writing?

LOCKRIDGE: Good journalism is good journalism whether consumer or B2B. Trade publications tend to be more devoted to "service journalism" — information, advice, and help in how readers can do jobs better and make businesses more successful. This isn't to say that B2B publications don't sometimes do some great news reporting and tough investigative features. Take a look at American Business Media's annual Jesse H. Neal award winners to get a feel for some of the best writing in the field. For instance, the 2011 best single article winner was for an article on swim coaches who are sexual predators.

More often, however, it's bread-and-butter stuff. For trucking, that means articles on topics such as the latest engine oil standards, how to improve your fuel economy, and the newest truck models, other new equipment, and product announcements.

There is a fine line to walk when it comes to editorial integrity. Because the companies you are writing about are frequently the same ones that are advertising prospects, this can be a challenge. Some B2B companies, such as the ones that are members of ABM, believe strongly in [keeping advertising separate from articles]. Others, unfortunately, are happy to promise advertisers coverage in exchange for ads.

B2B publications also typically run leaner staffs than consumer pubs. Personally, I like this because I've found it gives me the opportunity to get involved in a wider variety of work. It also means good freelancers can be very valuable.

Q: What sort of opportunities are there for freelancers in writing for trade magazines?

LOCKRIDGE: It depends on the magazine, of course, but I have depended on freelancers to various degrees at every trade magazine I've worked for. There are some opportunities to pitch story ideas, but generally trade magazines work from an editorial calendar, and we are more likely to be looking for someone willing to take on assignments.

I once had a freelancer who did some work for me at both the farming magazine and my first trucking magazine. He sold me a story about a traveling circus, about the logistics and challenges of using trucks to move from town to town. He spent several days with the circus and had also sold stories to a number of other trade magazines, such as one about the animal care to a veterinarian magazine and one about how you feed all the performers to a food service magazine. So he made multiple sales from one trip.

Q: What tips would you give to writers who want to write for trade publications?

LOCKRIDGE: Because much of the writing for trade publications is technical in nature, you may be able to break in with a personality profile or case study. Is there a company or professional you know who is doing something innovative or is particularly successful? Chances are there's a trade magazine devoted to their field.

Like any freelance job, make sure to research the publication you want to submit to. This is easier than ever with the Internet. B2B publications almost all have websites, and many have digital archives so you can get an idea of the type of articles they write. There may be an editorial calendar online, so you can pitch your idea to fit in with their plans.

When making a pitch, tell the editor what experience you have writing about that field, or if you don't have any, tell the editor about how you have successfully covered topics in the past that were unfamiliar to you.

Let them know that you're willing to accept assignments. I keep a file of freelancers who have contacted me in case I have something come up in their area that they may be able to cover for me.

Q: What does the future look like for trade publications?

LOCKRIDGE: Savvy B2Bs are developing a strong online presence. We have websites, blogs, a mobile phone and iPad app, and Twitter and Facebook, and are getting into video.

Everyone wonders about the future of magazines. The Internet has decimated daily papers. But magazines offer a more in-depth experience than newspapers. I believe they will persevere, at least until someone develops an electronic version that is portable and affordable. There are some B2Bs that have gone entirely digital. The viability of that depends partly on your audience. (It's a lot easier to throw a magazine in the cab of a truck than find a good wireless connection on the road.) But no matter what medium the information is presented in, businesses will still need that information to be successful.

A couple of associations that are good for more information include American Business Media, which is an association of corporate members; and the American Society of Business Publication Editors, which is an association of individual writers and editors. These are both really good resources for writers interested in the trade field. ✍

Deborah Lockridge is Editor-in-Chief of *Heavy Duty Trucking*, which provides information on what trucking fleet executives need to know to run their business, including equipment selection and maintenance, government regulations, and industry and business trends.

through the research and information you use.

3. They are written with a casual, yet knowledgeable style.

Trade magazines are a good blend of professional journals and consumer magazines. Your style of writing thus needs to be a blend of the kinds of writing you'd see in the pages of those types of publications. Provide lots of good information, but don't go overboard with big words and technical jargon. Along with the information, include people, quotations, and interesting details so that your article doesn't sound like a research paper.

Even if you are not now familiar with trade magazines, they offer many writing opportunities if you are willing to invest the time to learn about them.

Exercises

1. Locate trade magazines online or at your local library or bookstore. Look through a copy of one of the magazines and take notes on the style of writing and topics it publishes.

2. Look at the list of trade magazines in *Writer's Market*. List 10 categories for which you would be interested in writing.

a.

b.

c.

d.

e.

f.

g.

h.

i.

j.

3. Consider your expertise, experiences, professional background, and interests. Based on them, list five specific industries that you would be qualified to write about.

    a.

    b.

    c.

    d.

    e.

4. Take the list of 10 categories you made for Exercise 2. Look through such sources as your local newspaper, Chamber of Commerce directory, staff directory of a local university, and telephone Yellow Pages and identify at least one individual who could serve as an expert for a story in each of those 10 categories of magazines.

    a.

    b.

    c.

    d.

    e.

    f.

    g.

    h.

    i.

    j.

5. Select one of the 10 categories of magazines you listed in Exercise 2, check the *Writer's Market* information for a magazine in one of the categories, and write a Letter of Introduction to the magazine's editor.

The Magazine Article

WHAT YOU WILL LEARN IN THIS CHAPTER

• Magazines are filled with articles on every topic imaginable. You need to become well acquainted with the topics and types of articles magazines publish and then decide what types you want to write.

• The most prevalent types of articles are how-to, informational, personality profiles, interviews, personal experience, investigative, roundup, historical, travel articles, humor, opinion, and shorts.

• Articles consist of three parts: a beginning, middle, and end. They are called the lead, body, and conclusion. The body is usually written in either a narrative or topical structure.

In the many magazines on my bedside table — or at my favorite online sites — I can read articles on scores of different topics. They capture my interest, make me laugh, teach me about something I never knew before, inspire me, introduce me to fascinating characters, take me to faraway places and unknown ones nearby, and touch me in many other ways.

Articles come in wide varieties and styles. Examples are stories such as the following:

"Creative Ideas for Water Gardens" (*Sunset* magazine)

"The South's Best Dog Parks" (*Southern Living*)

"Discover Yoga's Stress Relieving Benefits" (*Health and Fitness*)

"Quiz: Are You Approachable?" (*Cosmopolitan*)

"Inside the NYPD's Special Victims Division" (*Newsweek*)

"Sticks and Stones: Keys to Prevent Bullying" (*Living with Teenagers*)

"Norway: Land of the Midnight Sun" (*National Geographic Traveler*)

"Are You Afraid of Your Cell Phone Now?" (*Salon*)

"An Evening at the Waldorf" (*Gourmet*)

"Riding Out the Storm: The 1900 Galveston Hurricane" (*History Magazine*)

"It's a Wonderful Midlife" (*Parade*)

"Double Blessings: Actress Patricia Heaton's Secrets to Success" (*Guideposts*)

This group of articles provided detailed, in-depth reporting (*Newsweek*'s inside story of the New York police department), entertained with a quick and fun quiz (*Cosmo*), inspired me to think about the future in a new way (*Parade*'s unique take on the midlife "crisis"), helped me be a better parent (*Living with Teenagers*'s with bullying-prevention tips), took a current news event and made it apply to my life (*Salon*'s story about cell phones' link to cancer), and took me on an armchair trip to Europe (*National Geographic Traveler*'s travelogue to Norway).

The articles ran the gamut from how-to pieces, to personality profiles, to travel pieces, to informational stories, to short fillers, to historical pieces. They epitomize the variety of articles in magazines today.

As a freelance feature writer, you will write articles on such topics as these — travel, gardening, childcare, hobbies, sports, news ... anything under the sun that you can come up with on your own or be assigned. And you will find yourself writing different types of articles — how-tos, profiles, news ... all of those types just mentioned above.

To be a successful freelance writer, you must start at the beginning stage and acquaint yourself with the magazine article. You must understand the ins-and-outs of the magazine industry so that you can equip yourself to produce the types of articles that editors want.

Types of Articles

As a freelancer, you can write numerous types of articles that editors want. Just look again in the pages of magazines, and you will find a wide variety of topics covered in a variety of ways. You see informational articles about health issues, how-to articles on saving money, travel pieces on summer vacations, personality profiles on celebrities, humor pieces on life as a parent. The options truly are endless ... which is why there is always a need for magazine writers.

Let's examine the types of articles you could write. As you read about them, consider the ones you would enjoy writing or that you feel especially equipped to write.

How-to Articles

One primary reason people read magazines — or newspapers, or websites, or nonfiction books — is to learn how to do something. Most magazines strive to provide information that will make readers' lives easier, more productive, less stressful, or more enriching. How-to articles fill this need by providing step-by-step, usually simple, information for readers.

Open the magazine closest to you, and chances are you will quickly find a how-to article. Such articles tell readers how to do almost anything, from how to lose weight, to how to improve job productivity, to how to encourage their child's productivity, to how to save money at the grocery store, to how to make their marriage stronger.

Most freelancers should consider writing how-to stories. They are some of the easiest to research and write, simply because they are usually straightforward and not too complex. Most of us can tell someone how to do something. Everyone has an expertise — and if you don't, you can interview someone who does. Therefore, material for a how-to article can come from personal experience or from interviewing an expert on the topic.

Although how-to articles are easy to write, that does not mean that they should not be written well. Even with a simple idea, you should be challenged to write about it in a way that a reader will find entertaining. You want to enhance your how-to piece with an interesting lead, good anecdotes, and strong examples.

A story on something you might consider bland or even "boring" — such as saving money at the gas pump, for example — can still be presented in an interesting way that will both help and entertain the reader.

Informational (or Service) Articles

Informational articles are closely related to how-to pieces. Both types provide readers with useful information. Informational articles don't, though, focus on how readers can do something but provide them with a storehouse of knowledge about a particular subject. (By the way, our English word "magazine" is derived from the French *magazin*, which came from the Arabic *makhzan*, which means "storehouse.") Informational articles provide a whole slate of information about a topic — roses, breast cancer, Tuscan wineries, marathons, etc. — by providing the traditional 5 W's learned in journalism training (the who, what, when, where, why, and how of a topic).

Informational articles require research because they must provide as much detail about the topic as possible. They should include good quotes, up-to-date statistics, resource information, and true-life examples.

These articles may not seem to be the most exotic to write, but magazines eat them up! They are worth learning how to do. You can make them interesting by selecting topics that particularly appeal to you and by using effective stylistic devices.

With informational articles, accompanying sidebars can be especially helpful. Sidebars make the articles even more marketable. They provide supplementary information on your topic. Editors find them especially appealing. An article on autism, for example, could include sidebars on resource websites, warning signs in young children, and a real-life story of an adult with autism.

Personality Profiles (or Interviews)

People love to read about other people, which accounts for the popularity of personality profiles and interviews in most magazines. Profiles and interviews focus on one of two types of people: *celebrities* (actors, musicians, athletes, business people, leaders, or well-known people in certain fields) or *ordinary people* who have done something out-of-the-ordinary — people who have been through a crisis and come out stronger, have an unusual hobby, have achieved great success, have a special expertise, or make a special difference in other people's lives. The people who are the focus of these stories are people who, in one way or another, will make an impression on readers. They will inspire or teach or entertain them in some way.

These articles are usually written in either of two ways. As profiles, they include information from the individual who is the focus of the article and interviews with friends, family members, colleagues, and anyone else who can add something to the article. As interviews, they contain information only from the person being profiled. Interviews can be presented in a "question and answer" format, or the information from an interview can be incorporated in a narrative structure.

Personal Experience Pieces

The old adage "Write what you know" certainly applies to feature writers. Many magazines will pay for what you know and what you have experienced in the form of personal experience articles and essays.

In thinking about your experiences or things you know about especially well, you should consider if they are things that magazine readers could benefit from. With what aspect of your experience can other people identify? Was it an experience that was especially eye-opening, inspiring, harrowing, humorous, even unbelievable? Is your special knowledge something that can make a difference in the lives of your readers? Can they identify with your feelings or learn how to improve their lives from reading about your experience and/or knowledge?

You can write about personal experiences in the three following ways:

1. As a narrative story based solely on your experience

Example: an article about your first-person experience traveling to Disney World

2. As part of a larger article on a particular topic

Example: a how-to piece on taking care of elderly parents, using your own experiences as a springboard for the article

3. As an essay based on a personal experience

Example: an essay about your experiences cooking as a child with your grandmother

Exposé or Investigative Articles

Some articles are written with the intent to investigate or expose an issue that needs to be delved into, in order to provide readers with much needed information. An exposé could be a general article on something such as the risk of cell phone use or the hazards of online dating — or it might be a more specific exposé on a particular person, company, location, or newsworthy issue.

General investigative pieces are more marketable to magazines than are more specific exposés, but there are markets for each of them. To identify a magazine, do your research on what individual magazines need.

In writing these types of articles, remember that you are doing a service for readers. Make your article as information-laden as possible. Don't make it an attack on someone. You are exposing or investigating something so that you can improve your reader's life. Remember also that you want to provide a balanced understanding of the topic. Do your best to get both sides of the story by talking to sources who can provide alternate views. In this way, you will give readers a balanced view and equip them to make their own decisions.

Roundup Pieces

Roundup articles focus on one theme, get information (such as quotes and statistics) from different sources, and then "round up the information" in an interesting way (often as a numbered list).

Examples of roundup pieces would be "20 Weight-Loss Tips from Fitness Experts," "12 Best Roller Coasters for Summer," and "7 Breakout Novelists You'll

Want to Read."

Roundup pieces are worthwhile from both the writer's and editor's standpoint. They are comparatively easy to research and write, and editors like them because they offer concise, informative fare in a way that is appealing to many readers.

Historical Articles

Many people are fascinated with the past. It's filled with colorful figures and important (and often surprising) events — and readers especially like to find out how the past is connected to their current life. Historical articles for magazines do just that. They tell about something important in the past and show how it relates to a reader's life today.

Historical articles can be written for general interest and popular consumer magazines, but can also be written for historically oriented magazines. They can be written narratively and chronologically or with a topical structure. However they are constructed, though, they need to be written in a way that makes events and characters interesting and relevant to today's readers.

A good way to present a historical topic is to tie it into a current event or a subject of contemporary interest. Look for events that will be celebrating 50th, 75th, 100th, or even 200th or 500th anniversaries.

Travel Pieces

Who doesn't like to read about a destination she has always dreamed of traveling to? Who doesn't want to get great tips about a place she will be visiting soon? Who doesn't like to learn about people, places, cultures, food, and experiences different than his own?

Travel pieces are found in a multitude of magazines. Travel magazines (such as *Conde Naste Traveler*, *Cruising*, and *RV Escape*) fill their pages with such articles, and both general interest and specialty magazines (such as women's, hiking, and wine magazines) that don't focus specifically on traveling still publish articles on travel and destinations.

Travel articles can be written in a variety of ways. Some of them are informational pieces with lots of practical details about a single destination or about several destinations with a common theme. Other articles are more personal, perhaps written as a travelogue or travel diary. Such articles are based on the writer's own experiences in visiting a place and interacting with its people, culture, food, and so forth. Travel articles are, obviously, more effective and entertaining when they are about a place you have visited. Research, then, will involve your own visits but can also include information from other sources, such as natives, travel experts, and other tourists.

When thinking about travel articles, consider why a certain place is special. What makes it unique? Why would other people want to read about it? How can you make it work for a specific magazine?

Humor Articles

Do you have a knack for finding the humor in situations? Do people tell you that you have a great sense of humor? Do you find yourself telling funny stories about things that have happened to you? If you can say "yes" to these questions, you might want to write humor articles or essays for magazines.

Humor articles have a comparatively limited market. Most magazines that publish them run them as one-page essays in a particular department or on a specific page (a back-page essay, for example). The trick in writing humor is to find the humor in common situations, so that your reader can relate to it. You must be able to inject humor into, for example, the family vacation or the job interview or the Thanksgiving dinner. Years ago, I wrote a humorous essay on my experience in buying a new bathing suit by thinking about how other women my age could relate to the "horror" of the situation.

Opinion

Many magazines publish one-page essays from a writer's perspective about a particular topic. Other magazines — such as news magazines, political publications, and online sites that deal with news and politics — publish numerous opinion articles. If you feel strongly about an issue and have a way of presenting your ideas in a compelling way, you may want to write opinion pieces.

If you want to get them published, though, they need to be interesting. Everyone has an opinion — but just because someone has an opinion doesn't mean that others want to read about it. Opinion pieces, while based on your own experiences and insights, need to be thoughtful and persuasive in a way that does not come across as egotistical, dogmatic, or uninformed. Back up your opinion with research and reasoned arguments. When someone reads your opinion piece and says something such as, "That writer knows what she's talking about," then you have probably supported your personal opinion with details that make sense and are well thought out. You have done your job — and you may, in fact, be on the way to persuading someone else to your side of an issue.

If you want to write opinion articles, a good way to get comfortable with them is to start by writing letters to the editor of your local newspaper. Most

Carolyn Tomlin
"Writing Inspirational Articles"

Q: How did you get started writing for magazines? And what do you work on primarily?

TOMLIN: I attended the LifeWay Writer's Conference [a conference organized by the publishing companies connected with the Southern Baptist denomination] in 1989 and came home with two writing assignments. My first published article came from that experience and was in *Living with Teenagers* magazine. Today, I usually average about 150 articles a year although in some years I have published as many as 300. I write primarily for religious and inspirational magazines, although I also write for several trade magazines.

Q: Why did you find yourself attracted to writing inspirational pieces?

TOMLIN: God has given me a strong sense of creativity, and using my five senses has always provided me with plenty of ideas that can be turned into inspirational articles. With the magazine market, a prolific writer reaches millions of readers annually. If a writer has a message, the magazine market is one of the best vehicles for contacting and reaching people.

Q: Where do you come up with your article ideas?

TOMLIN: Ideas are everywhere! Listen to conversations. Read newspapers and listen to the media for local, state, and world news for ideas and trends. Then, research and interview people to turn these ideas into articles. Whenever I accept an assignment, I ask God to guide me and to help me write an article that will help others.

Q: What were the greatest challenges you faced in first getting published?

TOMLIN: It was time. Teaching full time, writing was simply my avocation. Now, it is my vocation. Also, keeping a balance in everything I do is a great challenge.

---

newspapers welcome well written letters on issues of the day, for letters to the editor are some of the most popular parts of many newspapers. Many people write letters to the editor on a regular basis, and they get countless responses. Starting out with letters is a good way to get experience with opinion writing before submitting to larger magazine markets.

Q: If you were starting all over, what would you wish you'd known more about?

TOMLIN: When I started writing, I didn't know any local writers. In fact, I spent hours in the library reading writing magazines and making copies of articles — just to learn the basic information. A local writing group, composed of some experienced writers, would have been a blessing.

Q: What writing advice would you give aspiring writers and students?

TOMLIN: Believe in yourself. God has given you talents that you aren't aware of. Use these and He will bless you with immeasurable gifts. I find joy in writing. It's all in your attitude. When you see time spent writing as a period of quiet and peace, you don't consider it work. Also find ways to mentor aspiring writers. Share what you have learned with others.

Q: What marketing advice would you give?

TOMLIN: I believe that marketing and writing have a 50/50 ratio. Making contacts, networking with editors, researching new markets — they require as much, or more, time as the actual writing.

Q: What specific tips or ideas do you have for writers especially interested in writing religious/inspirational pieces?

TOMLIN: Start with your own denomination, but include other religious/inspirational magazines. Most denominations have magazines that focus on families, children, youth, leadership, missions and others. These magazines need writers who can show God's love to the world. Write for a sample copy. Study these magazines and write a query letter for a forthcoming issue.

Carolyn Tomlin has had more than 3,600 articles published in a variety of magazines. Most of them are religious or inspirational in nature (such as *Open Windows*, *Home Life*, *Lutheran Digest*, and *Christian Leadership*).

Short Pieces and Fillers

Look through the pages of most magazines, and you will find at least three or four lengthy feature articles. They are usually in the "well" — or center — of the magazine. But you'll see an even greater number of short pieces and fillers. They can be anything from departments and columns on particular topics, to recipes, quizzes, lists, and tips.

Common Short Pieces
Published in Magazines

Types of short articles and fillers that are found in magazines:

1. Columns & Departments
2. Lists
3. Tips
4. Quizzes
5. Mini-profiles
6. Devotionals
7. Travel shorts
8. Games & puzzles
9. Crafts
10. Reviews (book, movie, restaurant, product, event, website)
11. Recipes

Editors love to get good ideas and submissions for short pieces — simply because they don't get enough of them. Freelance writers often think of submissions for full-length articles, but few think of writing shorter pieces. Set yourself apart, then, and submit ideas for these pieces. To find markets, simply note the needs of the magazines in *Writer's Market* or the writing guidelines for the magazines. Editors will let you know what types of short pieces they need.

Writing an 1,800-word article is one thing. Writing a 250-word column is another altogether. In fact, the short piece is often more difficult to write because you have to practice brevity and restraint. You have to pick your information wisely and then write your article in a constrained, smart way. Writing short pieces, then, is not always easy — even though it may seem so until you try it. The *Writing Advantage* feature "Common Short Pieces Published in Magazines" on this page lists the various types of short pieces that magazines publish.

The *Writing Advantage* feature "Article Types" on page 45 provides a handy list of types of magazine articles. Refer to it in deciding what you want to write.

At the end of this chapter you will find a sample how-to article, a sample travel article, and a sample humor article. Along with accompanying exercises, they will help you understand better how such articles work.

Article Types

Types of feature articles that can be written for magazines:
1. How-to articles
2. Informational (or service) articles
3. Personality profiles (or interviews)
4. Personal experience pieces
5. Exposes or investigative pieces
6. Roundup pieces
7. Historical articles
8. Travel articles
9. Humor essays
10. Opinion pieces
11. Short items

Today's Most Popular Topics

So you now know the types of articles you can write, and you may have actually begun to think of which types you would like to write. Most people instinctively know that they would enjoy writing how-to pieces — or if they would dislike doing so.

What types of topics, though, can you write about in your how-to article or personal experience piece? What subjects do magazine readers — and editors — want to read about?

Think about the magazines you read on a regular basis. What topics do they cover?

No matter the type of magazines you read, you can probably think quickly of the topics you see on a regular basis.

If you read women's magazines, you will find articles on beauty, fashion, relationships, sex, diet, self-help, and celebrities.

If you read religious magazines, you will find articles on topics such as the Bible, faith, relationships, church, social issues, prayer, and inspiring people.

If you read food magazines, you will find articles on specific foods, chefs, restaurants, cooking trends, health, and cooking techniques.

Most freelancers who have written for several years have published articles about literally hundreds of topics. I have written about topics I know a lot about, but also topics that were new to me. I have written on personal topics but also on professional ones. I have written about things you see every day and topics that are unique. Gardens, dental care, real estate, cupcakes, authors, the Civil War, Earth Day, bathing suits, Halloween costumes, missionaries, bulimia, kite-flying, self-esteem, coupons, listening, brain development, Texas, wineries, Helen Keller, water parks, premature birth, tornadoes, college football — these are some of the topics that I've covered ... and the list goes on, and on, and on, and ON. That may seem like a lot of different topics — but freelancers write about almost everything.

What is the main point here?

It is to show that magazines publish articles on literally ANY topic you can think of. The topics you can write about are limited only by the ones that can be imagined. Magazine readers voraciously read about anything and everything ... and everything in between.

The trick is to determine what you want to write about — what you feel needs to be said — and find a magazine that is interested in the same thing. Thus, you can make sure your specific idea on that topic is marketable. Chapter 8 in this book covers the marketing aspect of magazine writing in more detail.

What Does a Magazine Article Look Like?

Chapter 11 in this book will go into detail about the structure of a magazine article, but at this point it's still important to have a rudimentary understanding of what a magazine article looks like.

A magazine article has three parts — as does every piece of writing, whether it's a television script, a report, a sermon, a brochure, or a song. They are the following: (1) a beginning, (2) a middle, and (3) an end. Let's consider each part in more detail.

1. The beginning of a magazine article is called the *lead*, and it is where you introduce your story in a way that quickly captures readers' attention. You want to draw your readers into the story right off the bat and make them want to keep reading to learn more.

Thus, the lead should be written in an interesting way. It can use any number of creative techniques. Some of the most effective techniques include the following:

- Presenting an anecdote (that is, a brief story)
- Describing a scene
- Asking interesting questions
- Making a startling (or otherwise interesting) statement
- Using a revealing quote

While your lead needs to be interesting enough to capture the readers' attention, it is of utmost importance that it relates to the theme of the article. It must adequately lead into the article's topic and theme. It must not be catchy just for the sake of being catchy. It must tell what the story is going to be about.

2. The middle section of the magazine article is called the *body*. It is where the meat of the action takes place and all the necessary information is presented.

The body is structured in one of two ways, depending on the type of article and what works best for the topic. The following are the two structures:

- Narrative (story)
- Topical (thematic)

An article written in a *narrative* structure presents the information in a story-telling fashion. It usually is structured chronologically, with a situation presenting itself, intensifying, and then being resolved. It can tell a story of a person's life or the chronology of a historical event, about your own experiences in a story style or about a travel destination in a narrative fashion. In fact, the narrative structure lends itself to any topic that takes place chronologically.

An article written in a *topical* structure presents its information by breaking the topic down into different sub-topics. This structure works particularly well with how-to and informational articles. By explaining a topic by its various points — sometimes indicated by subheads, numbers, or bullets — the information can be presented in a straightforward, easy-to-comprehend manner.

3. The final part of an article's construction is its ending. In magazine articles, the ending is called the *conclusion*. It must wrap up the article in a satisfying way. It leaves the reader with the last, lingering thought on the article's subject. You don't want an article to end abruptly or simply fade away. The conclusion hammers home the point of the article. Thus, it must relate to the article's central theme. Because of the importance of the conclusion, you should spend adequate time to create one that is satisfying to the reader.

Some of the most effective ways to construct a conclusion include the following:

- Finishing with a good quote
- Presenting a well-written wrap-up of the article's information
- Tying the conclusion back into the lead paragraph. If, for example, the lead paragraph uses a description, write another, related description for the conclusion. If questions are asked in the lead, answer them in the conclusion.

It's particularly important to realize that the conclusion is not something you just tack onto the end of your article. It should not merely summarize or repeat. It should be thematic and memorable.

Chapter 11 in this book will provide detailed instruction on writing each of these three parts of a magazine feature article. At this point, though, it's important to understand that being able to handle the construction of an article properly is necessary if you want to succeed as a freelance writer.

Exercises

1. Choose copies of five different magazines. Identify the types of articles you see. Make a list of them.

2. From the five magazines you selected for Exercise 1, make a list of the topics the articles cover.

3. Read the how-to article "Back to School Success" on pages 50-53 in this book. Make a list of the information you gained from reading it. Then write a paragraph on how the writer presented the information. How could you make the article better?

4. Read the travel article "Where Miracles Happen" on pages 53-54 in this book. Write a paragraph on how the writer presented the information. How could you make the article better?

5. Read the humor article "Retiring Will Come Easy for This Duke" on pages 55-56 in this book. Write a paragraph on how the writer structured the story. How could you make the article better?

6. Select one of your favorite magazines and analyze the types of articles in it. How many of each of the following types does it include?

Name of magazine: _____

____ How-to articles

____ Informational (or service) articles

____ Personality profiles (or interviews)

____ Personal experience pieces

____ Exposés or investigative pieces

____ Roundup pieces

____ Historical articles

____ Travel articles

____ Humor essays

____ Opinion pieces

____ Short items

7. From the previous question, select the two articles you think are most effective and the two you think are least effective. Write one paragraph about each of the four articles explaining your assessment of each.

Sample Articles

Read each of the following sample articles and then answer the questions about it at the end.

How-to Article

Back to School Success:
Creating a Strong Parent-Teacher Relationship

"Do you think I'll like my new teacher, Mom?" "Whose class am I going to be in?"

As the new school year rolls around, these are some of the questions you probably hear quite often in your household. Children can't wait to find out who their teacher will be for the new school year, and then they eagerly anticipate getting to know that teacher.

Parents have similar concerns, although their questions may be a little bit different. Their questions about their child's teacher might sound something like these: "What type of teacher will she be?" "How will the personalities of my child and her teacher work well together?" "Will he communicate well with the parents?"

Your child's success in school is directly tied to his or her teacher — and, more specifically, the way you work with that teacher. Open communication and active involvement with your child's teacher can make the year go smoothly and can create an effective environment for your child's learning. Research studies have, in fact, concluded that children do better in school when parents talk often with teachers and become involved in the school.

According to a pamphlet produced by the National Association of Elementary Principals and distributed by the Boise School District, "much of what teachers are hoping for has to do with communication." It's important, then, to get off on the right foot as the new school year begins.

There are many ways to foster a wonderful relationship with the teachers at your son or daughter's school. Keep these tactics in mind:

Get to know the teacher right away. There is no time like right now when it comes to creating strong lines of communication with your child's teacher. Introduce yourself to the teacher as soon as possible, in whatever venue the school allows (there might be, for example, a registration day or a "get to know the teacher" day at the beginning of the year; if not, send a note to your child's teacher on the first day of school).

Volunteer and get involved. Do what you can to get involved in your child's school and classroom, and let your teacher know what you are willing and want to do. There are many opportunities — everything from serving as the official room mother, to helping with class parties, to being a PTA officer, to (if you are a working mother) putting papers together or organizing a phone tree in the evenings.

Attend parent events. Schools offer plenty of opportunities to meet teachers and learn more about your child's progress, but you must actually attend them to reap their benefits. Be sure to attend Open Houses, PTA meetings, and other parental activities offered by the school.

Stay connected. Find out the best way to stay in touch with your child's teacher, and then utilize those avenues. If there is a notebook that comes home every night with information, check it daily; if there is a school website that lets you keep in touch with your child's teacher and specific class, check it often; if the teacher answers emails, keep in touch that way as well. Gifted Education teacher Jill Hickey says that email is always better than a phone call, and she also stresses that parents need to let teachers know the best way to keep in contact. "Give correct contact information to your teacher, and keep it up-to-date," she says.

Keep up with class activities. The Boise School District encourages parents to know what is going on in their child's classroom. "If the teacher sends home regular updates on what the class is studying, read them," it recommends. "Also ask your child, 'What are you working on now?' Look at your child's books, and see what topics the class is covering."

Show your appreciation. Gretchen Hanna, Washington mom of two high schoolers, says that she always makes a point of telling teachers that she appreciates their hard work. "I try always to thank them for their hard work at the end of any email I might send them — whether I've asked them for something or not," she says. Sarah Cox, mother of three daughters, tries to do something special for the teacher when she can. "I like to take fresh baked muffins and fresh flowers for their desk," she says, "to let them know that I am thinking of them as a person, not just a teacher."

Inform your teacher of any special concerns. It's important to keep your child's teacher informed of anything (inside or outside the classroom) that might affect your child's school performance. "Tell them when something is going on that could affect the child's physical or emotional state," Hickey says. The Boise School District concurs. "If you notice your child is struggling with school work, or if she's bothered by other students — or the teacher — contact the teacher right away," it says. "The earlier you step in, the quicker things can be set right, and the sooner your child can get back on track."

Provide at-home support for the teacher. Be sure that you are positive toward your child's teacher at home; support her rules and expectations with your child. Use positive words and model positive actions, so that your child will return to school with a similarly positive outlook.

By utilizing such tactics, you can answer your child's questions and assuage any fears she might have about the new school year. In doing so, you can also build a strong relationship with your child's teacher as well.

(This article originally appeared in *Treasure Valley Family* magazine. Written by Cheryl Wray.)

Questions

1. What technique does the article's lead use?
2. What structure is used for the body of the article?
3. How are the article's main points spelled out for the reader?
4. How many and what types of sources does the article use?
5. What techniques best provide the reader with the information he needs?
6. What technique does the article's conclusion use?
7. What makes this article effective as a how-to piece?
8. What changes might make the article more effective?

Travel Article

Where Miracles Happen: Helen Keller's Ivy Green

The modest white house seems typical of many found throughout the South, with its inviting front porch, beautiful interior, and lovely grounds. But those physical attributes hint nothing at the miracle that took place here more than a century ago.

Walk around to the back lawn, though, and there sits the evidence — the black water pump where blind and deaf Helen Keller first understood the concept of language in 1887. It was here that Keller's teacher, Annie Sullivan, signed the word W-A-T-E-R into the 7-year-old girl's hand while cool water from the pump flowed over her other hand. The idea finally clicked, and Keller signed the word back. By the end of the day, she had learned 30 words.

The pump is just one of the historical features found at Ivy Green, Helen Keller's birthplace in the intimate, inviting northwest Alabama town of Tuscumbia (pop. 7,856). The home includes a museum filled with Keller documents and artifacts (including her complete collection of Braille books), original furnishings and photographs, an adjoining cottage where Sullivan and Keller lived for two weeks in isolation from the rest of the family, a carriage house, landscaped grounds, and an outdoor theater. William Gibson's world-famous play, "The Miracle Worker," is performed by local actors there each Saturday and Sunday evening throughout late June and July.

For Keller Johnson, Helen Keller's great-great-niece, Ivy Green's appeal comes from that sense of living history.

"Ivy Green is not just an old house," Johnson says. "You can actually come here and see the water pump. There aren't many historical sites where you can see history so vividly."

Johnson, a lifelong resident of Tuscumbia, serves as the vice president of the Helen Keller Foundation, which supports laboratory and clinical research to advance vision and hearing worldwide and holds programs of public education on Helen Keller's legacy. She also works with the American Foundation for the Blind.

Johnson says she often walks the grounds of Ivy Green and visualizes how life must have been for Keller and her sister — Johnson's great-great-grandmother, Mildred. "You can just imagine Helen and Mildred playing in these big trees, much like sisters would do today," she says. "Anyone who has read Helen's biography or other books about her can do the same thing. They can see the stories come to life here at Ivy Green."

Before Annie Sullivan came to teach Keller, the child's life was out of control. She felt helpless and hopeless, as did her parents. But that day at the water pump indeed changed her life. In six months, Keller knew 625 words; by the time she was 16, she spoke well enough to attend preparatory school.

"This young girl from Tuscumbia not only learned how to read, using her hands, but she went on to learn speech, attend school, and eventually graduate from Radcliffe College," says Sue Pilkilton, Ivy Green director.

Keller embarked on a career that educated and inspired millions. She lectured in more than 25 countries on five continents, wrote five books, and brought new courage to blind and sighted people alike. (Visit www.helenkeller-foundation.org for more information.)

Johnson has devoted her life to carrying on her ancestor's legacy by educating children across Alabama about disability issues. Part of that education comes from the annual Helen Keller Festival — held each year on the last weekend in June — where kids can learn Braille and sign language. Highlights of the festival include a juried arts and crafts show, parade, athletic events, and street concerts by national and local musicians.

Residents of Tuscumbia are proud of its designation as home of America's "First Lady of Courage." Helen Keller's presence, in fact, pervades the town.

"Tuscumbia is one of those small towns that thrives on its past, but is not stuck in the past," Johnson says. "We are proud of Helen Keller and what she means to our town. We also, though, continue to thrive and grow."

Pilkilton says the town and the many Helen Keller sites at Ivy Green continue to draw visitors from around the world. She says those visitors, in exploring the house and walking the grounds, leave with a better sense of Keller's personal life and lasting legacy.

(This article originally appeared in *American Profile*. Written by Cheryl Wray.)

Questions

1. What is the article's theme?
2. How does the title relate to the theme of the article?
3. What technique does the article's lead use?
4. How does the article use description to place the topic in its setting?
5. What research did the writer do?
6. How many and what types of sources does the article use?

7. What structure is used for the body of the article?

8. How does the conclusion tie back to the lead?

9. What changes might make the article more effective?

Humor Article

Retiring Will Come Easy for This Duke

After 38 years of college teaching, I've decided to retire.

Some of my friends ask me if it will be hard to retire. I tell them, "How hard can it be? After all, it shouldn't be that difficult to transition from doing nothing to doing nothing."

Thinking, though, that I should have something to do in retirement, I asked my brother, a retired English professor, what he would advise. He told me, very succinctly for a professor: "Piddle."

I thought I should get a second opinion. So I asked my wife's cousin, who is retired from the railroad, what he advises. "Some days," he explained to me, "you will have things that are urgent and need to be done that very day, and you must decide whether to do them or to take a nap. Always take the nap."

That seems easy enough, but I still thought I was in need of something. While cleaning out my campus office, I came across a certificate that reminded me that Fob James, when he was governor, appointed me to the position of "Alabama Colonel" 15 years ago. Now that, I thought, has some potential.

So I called the governor's office in Montgomery and inquired.

"That's *honorary* Alabama Colonel," the secretary told me.

Then, in answer to some questions from me, she informed me, "No, there's no salary.... No, you don't get to whack people with billy clubs."

I was disappointed. That seemed to be the end of any good retirement prospects for me.

But fortunately, as if by providence, Prince William and Kate, the newlyweds, were touring in Hollywood. I've never been impressed with royalty — because being a king or queen or prince or duchess is just an accident of birth. For example, I could just as easily have been born as Prince Charles as he could. Then I could live in castles I didn't pay for and wear plumed hats that no ordinary, self-respecting man would dare put on.

My wife, though, is a different matter. She loves the British royalty. Her favorite movies are *The Queen*, *The King's Speech*, *The Last King* and *King Kong*.

Besides, her family name is Stuart, and she reminds me frequently that she is descended from the House of Stuart, kings of Great Britain and Ireland. She still thinks the American Revolution was a mistake, and, when she is piqued at me, she hurls at me the worst insult she can think of. She smirks slowly, disdain oozing in every syllable: "You Yaaan-keeee Doooo-dle."

Despite what my wife considers my humble origins, actually *my* being a member of royalty always has secretly appealed to me. So I figured that an ideal retirement activity would be to be royalty.

So I took up genealogical research — and, would you believe it, I am descended from kings and queens of Denmark and Sweden? No kidding! This is true!

I won't provide here all the evidence and documentation, but one of my ancestors — Walter Giffard (Walterus Giffard de Longueville) — accompanied William the Conqueror in the Norman invasion of England in 1066. William titled him the first Earl of Buckingham. I pointed out to my wife that that was LONG before the Stuarts were around.

So now I've decided deinitely what to do in retirement. I'm going to be David, Duke of Buckingham.

Being royalty has many benefits. Yesterday, my wife asked me to carry out the trash.

"Dukes," I told her, "don't do that."

(This article originally appeared in the *Birmingham News*. The author has requested that his name not be used.)

Questions

1. What is the theme of the article?
2. How does the title set the tone for the article?
3. What is the first humorous line in the article?
4. Pick out the joke you like best in the article. What technique does it use for its humor?
5. Although this article is told in first-person, it uses a number of sources. What or who are they?
6. What structure is used for the body of the article?
7. How does the conclusion relate to the theme of the article?
8. What changes might make the article more effective?

The Feature Writer
and the Writing Process

WHAT YOU WILL LEARN IN THIS CHAPTER

• Some feature writers work full-time, and others write as moonlighters or part-timers. Some work on a publication staff, and others are contributing writers or solely freelance writers.

• Successful freelancers consider accuracy, honesty, and non-bias vitally important. They practice creativity, specialization, professionalism, passion, persistence, and growth.

• The process of having an article published in a magazine is a systematic one. By following all the steps of the process, a writer has a good chance of having an article accepted and published.

• Twelve steps lead to success as a feature writer. The cycle begins with developing a marketable idea and ends with starting over with a new idea for a different magazine.

*W*hat does a magazine writer look like? What type of writers do magazine editors look for?

As you look for opportunities to write for magazines, these are important questions to ask. You must make sure you know what you are aspiring to do and what the nature of your work will be.

Let's start by looking at two real-life writers.

Ginny is a full-time freelance writer who started out by majoring in English in college. She then took specialized writing classes and attended writing conferences because she wanted to be a freelance writer for magazines. She began ac-

57

tively trying to get published in magazines by coming up with a specific marketing plan. For the first three months of her career, she sent out 25 query letters a week. Soon, she got the attention of several magazine editors. A teenage magazine accepted her first article idea, and it published her first article three months later.

Ginny became a regular columnist for that same teenage magazine. She also began writing regularly for several religious and inspirational magazines. In fact, she found that those two areas really were her niche. She soon knew that her passions were (1) writing for teenagers and (2) writing on inspiring topics.

Today, Ginny writes regularly for seven nationally known, high-circulation magazines. She also has segued into writing young adult fiction and is currently working on her third novel.

Mark is a high school science teacher. He has never had an article published in a national magazine, but he has published 500 articles in local and niche magazines on a variety of topics.

Mark has always loved writing and wanted to supplement his teaching salary by informing and entertaining other people about science and technology issues. When he discovered a slate of magazines published at local universities, he queried several editors and soon received a number of article assignments. He now writes for those local magazines as well as for several children's and men's magazines on technology and environmental topics — all while continuing his work as a teacher.

Mark says he lives the best of both worlds. He has two jobs he loves, one of which encourages the creativity for which he never had found an outlet before.

Writers like Ginny and Mark are everywhere. They have an expertise and passion for particular subjects, and they have found a way to turn those interests into published credits and income.

Thousands of writers do the same thing. They write about travel or health-related topics. They write restaurant reviews for a local newspaper. They write for children or senior adults. They write for trade or business magazines. They write for online magazines. They write full-time, part-time, or as moonlighters.

All of these individuals are *freelance writers*. They are not on staff with a publication. Instead, they market and contract themselves independently to magazines, newspapers, and online publications.

In getting ready to submit articles to a magazine — or to live a life like Ginny or Mark — freelance writers first need to understand the nature of a publication's staff and how they will fit into it.

Magazines, newspapers, and online publications utilize the following types of writers:

• *Staff Writers*

Many publications have a number of staff writers who work in-house and full-time. They take assignments directly from editors and work with the resources the magazines allow.

• *Contributing Writers*

Most magazines also have contributors who write on a regular basis. They are not considered in-house, on-staff writers, but do write regularly (usually every issue) for the magazine. These writers are often experts in a particular area who are recognized by readers.

• *Freelance Writers*

Most publications, especially magazines, rely on freelance writers for a portion of their work. That means many opportunities exist for freelancers. Some publications use them sparingly, while others use them for the bulk of their content. Freelance writers are used on speculation, based on ideas that they propose to editors. Often, editors forge relationships with these freelancers and begin giving them assignments.

Some freelancers work full-time. Most, though, are people with regular non-writing jobs who "moonlight" as freelancers.

In this book, we will spend most of the time on freelance writing for magazines. However, the skills the book covers — such as structuring articles, writing leads, and developing writing style — will aid you if you should ever work as a staff or contributing writer.

Qualities of Professional Writers

All writers — whether they are on staff or freelance — should adhere to professional standards. The standards are those that the writing industry — the writing family, if you will — holds to be of utmost importance to the integrity of the craft and profession. Freelancers should always strive to embody these qualities and work in the truest spirit of professionalism. They must be professional even if they're working from home, querying an editor for the first time, conducting research, or submitting an article to a small magazine. Every writing project demands the highest standards.

Writers should adhere to the following standards:

• *Accuracy*

When people read your article, they believe what you say. They take you at your word for the facts and information in your article. It's vitally important, then, always to assure accuracy in your writing. In fact, accuracy is recognized as the most important element for professional writers. Schools of journalism, agencies, organizations, and writers themselves all place a premium on it. According to the Reuters News Agency's *Handbook of Style*, "Accuracy is at the heart of what we do. It is our job to get it first, but it is above all our job to get it right. Accuracy, as well as balance, always takes precedence over speed."

My husband was recently interviewed for an online magazine because of his work in coaching youth sports. When he saw the final article in print, he was dismayed because there were quotes attributed to him that he had never said. The ages of our children were also reported incorrectly. He groused, tongue-in-cheek, "I thought you journalists were supposed to get your facts right."

Such errors commonly show up in both newspaper and magazine articles. They remind us yet again of the importance of accuracy. No writer should misspell a name, misquote someone, or get the facts wrong. Aim, always, for "getting it right."

• *Honesty*

Instances of inaccuracy in journalism have resulted in a widely held belief that journalists are dishonest. In fact, the Pew Research Center for the People and the Press has reported various surveys that show that at least two-thirds of the American public don't believe what they read in newspapers.

Honesty, though, should be a hallmark of feature writing. We writers should get the facts straight, and we must also be honest in our storytelling. Readers should get the sense that we want what's best for them — that we are giving them an article that will inform, entertain, or inspire them truthfully. We want readers to believe us.

• *Non-bias*

Journalists are supposed to be unbiased toward the subject of a story — willing and eager to tell all sides of an issue or topic, putting their own opinions aside and instead reporting the facts.

While feature writing may not be as "hard hitting" as news reporting, it still must adhere to the philosophy that unbiased reporting and writing are critical.

For example, in researching a feature article on storm recovery after a tornado outbreak in the South in 2011, I found different views of the way FEMA was handling the process. For a balanced story, it was important to include the views of people who held differing opinions. That required talking to both FEMA officials and tornado victims.

Even in doing lighter pieces, be sure to get both sides of any issue. One of the best ways to counterbalance possible bias is simply by gathering as much information and talking to as many sources as you can. The more material you get about your topic, the better. If you've gained a thorough understanding, you will be better able to appreciate the nuances of your subject. That will influence the way you write about it, and your article will be more likely to come across as unbiased and fair.

The *Writing Advantage* feature "Accuracy Checklist" on page 62 lists a number of points dealing with honesty and accuracy. These points, recommended by the Society of Professional Journalists, are valuable for feature writers.

The Process of Getting an Article Published

Every success begins with a small step.

An athlete will tell you that his team can't win the big game if he and his teammates don't practice months before the season even starts.

A husband and wife celebrating 50 years of marriage will tell you that their success didn't start at year 30. The key to their marital success began when they were dating — and, even before, as they prepared to find the person they wanted to spend their lives with.

A successful businessman or woman will tell you that professional acclaim never just appears on their office desk. It doesn't fall like manna from heaven. The success is a result of learning, and experimenting, and planning, and implementing, and doing all the things the right way.

To put it even more simply, a small child doesn't just suddenly appear in the world already knowing how to eat, and talk, and respond, and read. It takes a lot of work — on the parent's part and also on the child's. My youngest daughter is becoming quite a reader. But she wasn't born knowing the ABC's, and she worked hard every day to go through the process ... learning her letters, then learning sounds, learning to put sounds together, and so on. Mastering reading takes time, but the reward is worth the effort.

Writing for magazines is much the same.

You must learn a particular process to have success at feature writing. You

Accuracy Checklist
Society of Professional Journalists

The Society of Professional Journalists (SPJ) recommends the following checklist of questions for writers. They focus primarily on the accuracy of facts.

1. Do you have a high level of confidence about the facts in your story and the sources that are providing them? If not, can you tell your story in a more accurate manner? If you have any doubts about your sources, can you delete them or replace them and achieve a higher likelihood of reliability?

2. Have you attributed or documented all facts?

3. Have you double-checked the key facts?

4. Can you provide the properly spelled name and accurate telephone number of every source cited?

5. Are you confident that all the factual statements in your story reflect the truth?

6. Are you prepared to defend publicly your fact checking and whatever other measures that were taken to verify your story?

7. Are the quotes in your story presented fairly, in context?

8. Are you quoting anonymous sources? Why are you using them? Are you prepared to defend publicly the use of those sources?

9. Are you using any material documents or pictures provided by anonymous sources? Why? What is your level of confidence about the validity of this material? Are you prepared to defend publicly the use of that material?

10. Have you described persons, minority groups, races, cultures, nations, or segments of society — e.g. business people, Vietnam veterans, cheerleaders — using stereotypical adjectives? Are such descriptions accurate and meaningful in the context presented?

11. Have you used potentially objectionable language or pictures in your story? Is there a compelling reason for using such information? Would the story be less accurate if that language or picture were eliminated?

12. Do your headlines (or broadcast promos or teasers) accurately present the facts and context of the story to which they are referring?

---

don't go to sleep one night wanting to have articles published and then wake up with your name in print. You must use the proper process to become a published writer.

It's important to realize, though, that succeeding as a writer is not the most difficult thing in the world. Writing and getting published are not brain surgery

— but they do require an understanding of and an adherence to a systematic process.

Nick Saban, one of today's most successful college football coaches, talks all the time about process. He says he teaches his players never to look ahead to tomorrow, never to look at the scoreboard during a game. He tells them to focus on what they can do at every step along the way of learning to be great football players. Then they will be prepared to win. "We simply focus on the process of being a champion," he has said.

To find success as a published writer, you must first realize that your eventual success begins by taking that first step. And then taking the next. And the next. "A journey of a thousand miles," a proverb says, "begins with a single step." It's like that song from the classic holiday cartoon *Santa Claus Is Coming To Town*. In one scene, the characters all sing together: "Put one foot in front of the other ... and soon you'll be walking out the door." Successful writing and publishing is a step-by-step process that takes effort and work — but you can accomplish it if you apply yourself.

How does this process work? Following is a step-by-step approach to getting published — starting with having the germ of an idea for an article to having the published article in one's excited hands.

It's a process that's easy to master — if you're dedicated to taking the time and making the effort necessary. You can be assured that it's a process that does lead to publishing success.

Note that these steps are the ones to take when submitting an article idea to an editor. They do not apply to writing an article that an editor has assigned.

1. Develop an idea that is marketable to a magazine(s).

All published freelance articles start with the germ of an idea. It may have come from a newspaper or magazine article, from a conversation, a personal experience, a topic you want to know more about, a billboard along the side of the road, just some random idea that came out of the blue, or any other source.

Take the idea and determine if it is a marketable idea. Will it interest a reader of a magazine? Is it a topic that is appropriate for a particular magazine? Would an editor like it? If you decide it is an idea that editors and readers would like, then go to the next step.

In developing ideas for feature articles, writers must consider the possibilities for *slanting* at particular magazines. With slanting, a writer can take one idea and develop it into two, three, or many more articles with different angles. Imagine, for example, that a writer develops an idea for a magazine article on how to save money at the grocery store during hard economic times. He would consider the various ways he could approach that topic for different magazines. By slanting the idea, he might propose the following articles:

- Saving money on meals — for food magazines
- Saving money on groceries during holidays — for retirement magazines
- Saving money by using coupons — for women's magazines
- Using grocery store shopping trips as a way to teach children about money management — for parenting magazines

Chapter 7 in this book will discuss generating ideas and slanting.

2. Do preliminary research so that you know enough to pitch your idea.

Once you have come up with an idea you think a magazine might want, do some preliminary research on the topic. The key to remember here is that you are *not* doing research to write an actual article yet. You simply want enough information to be able to write a good query letter in order to pitch your idea to an editor.

Begin looking for information on the article you're going to propose. If it's a how-to or informational article, go online and search for information. Do some research into possible sources you might use. If it happens to be a personal experience piece you want to write, start jotting down the main thoughts you want to include in the article.

Once you've done enough research to have a good grasp of the idea, write a rough outline. By this point, you should have enough information to propose the topic to an editor.

3. Locate magazines as possible markets for your idea (using Writer's Market and online writers guidelines).

If your goal is to be published, then the article idea can't just be any idea. It's got to be an idea that will develop into the type of article that will fit a specific publication. In fact, to increase your odds for getting published, you need to know that a variety of publications would be possible markets for your idea. The more magazines to which you can submit the idea, the better!

How do you locate possible markets? The best ways include the following:

- Knowing about the magazine field in general
- Using *Writer's Market*
- Using online writers guidelines
- Visiting magazine websites

• Keeping up-to-date on market changes

Chapter 8 in this book will discuss finding markets.

4. Write and submit query letters to multiple magazines.

Submitting a query letter to a magazine editor is the standard procedure for getting an article idea accepted for publication. The query letter is a one-page "quick sell" of your idea to the editor and consists of the following four parts:

• An attention-getting introduction
• The details of your article idea, which should be obviously slanted to the magazine
• Information about yourself
• A closing

You must provide the editor with a quick, yet thorough, understanding of your proposed idea. If done right, the query letter will make the editor *want* to see your article.

Query letters are vital in the publication process. They are a necessary part of how the magazine industry operates. Editors want to see query letters because — as compared to long articles — they save them time. Freelance writers, in the same way, write queries because they require less time than writing completed articles that may or may not find a home at a magazine.

E-queries have become popular with both writers and editors. They utilize the same format as a traditional query letter sent through regular mail.

Chapter 9 in this book will discuss query letters and e-queries.

5. Receive a go-ahead (a positive response) from a magazine,

Once you have submitted your query letter, you will wait with much anticipation for a response from the magazine editor. Don't sit around waiting, though, for the response. It may take some time. Magazines vary in their procedure for replying to writers, but you will receive some type of response. Some editors will respond to an e-query within a few days. Others may not respond for a month or longer.

You can expect to receive one of the following three responses:

• A rejection. The editor tells you "no."
The key with rejections is not to get discouraged and to realize that they can

Vicki Moss
"Writing for Kids' Magazines"

Q: How did you break into children's magazines?

MOSS: I first ventured into writing for children by writing middle grade novels, but I couldn't find any editors interested in my work (probably because a meeting with an agent scared me silly when I first began writing). So I decided to try to write for the magazine market after another writer told me she'd had success there. I did my homework and tried to read as many kids' magazines as I could to see what stories were selling.

I broke into the market with a story in rhyme, breaking the rules of agents and editors that said "Don't send rhyme unless you're a professional poet." At that time, I hadn't published any poetry, and yet my first published article was in rhyme. After that, I sold a story about an Australian roach named Dave. The editor put it in as the lead story in the "Bugs" issue. When the editor praised my work on that piece, it just made me want to keep sending in more stories.

Q: What is appealing to you about writing for kids?

MOSS: I suppose because in some ways I'm still a child at heart myself. When writing a story, I try to write articles I would have wanted to read when I was a child.

At first, I thought writing for children would be easy. It's not. Then it became a challenge. Did I really have what it takes to write a children's magazine article and then do it again, and again? Once I learned how to craft a 500-word article, it became so much fun to run my finger down a theme list and to ask myself about each theme, "Okay, what do I know about trucks, vacation fun, wagon trains, and snakes – SNAKES! ICK!" I did happen to know quite a bit about snakes, and what I didn't know I researched. That story about snakes that I wrote in a rhyming poem sold twice and was used on a teaching CD.

---

be learning tools. Try to determine what you did wrong, so that you learn from the rejection and don't make the same mistake again.

For most beginning writers, rejections are the most common response. As you learn the process, though, go-aheads will begin to outnumber rejections.

• A go-ahead. The editor wants to see your article.

A "go-ahead" is called that because it means that the editor has read your query letter and now wants you to "go ahead and send your article for us to look at." A go-ahead does not necessarily mean the magazine will publish your article, but it does assure you that the editor likes your idea, wants to see your article,

Q: What things do freelancers need to remember about writing for kids' magazines (as opposed to women's magazines and other general consumer magazines)?

MOSS: Kids love to be entertained. Try to incorporate humor when you can because those are the stories that will sell. Also, magazines are always needing puzzles and how-to articles. They will also take rhyming stories and poems if they are well written.

Q: What advice would you give aspiring writers/students who would like to write for the children's magazine market?

MOSS: Study each magazine. They usually all want something different. Get a copy either online or by snail mail of their theme lists. Once you have that, then you can go through and choose a theme.

Also, practice writing several articles that are 500 words long. It helps you learn how to write tight. If your article turns out to be 750 words, go back through the manuscript and cut the fat. Whittle it down until it's 500 words because those articles sell much easier than the longer articles (which increases your chances of breaking in).

Q: What marketing advice do you have for those same individuals?

MOSS: If you sell first North American rights only, then you can resell your articles elsewhere. I wanted to hold onto my rights so I could use the articles later. So I was choosy about whom I queried. I'm so glad I was selective because I was able to get paid several times for the same article.

Good luck to all who pursue this adventure. It's been very rewarding for me.

Vicki Moss has been published in such children's magazines as *Boys Quest* and *Hopscotch* and is the author of the book *How to Write for Kids' Magazines*. She is Editor-at-Large of *Southern Writers Magazine*.

and then will make a decision. Realize that this is a typical way for editors to deal with freelancers and that, if you get a go-ahead, you are close to getting a publication.

• A firm assignment. In response to your query letter, the editor assigns you to write the article with a specific deadline.

6. Research, write, and edit your article.

At this point, you will get serious with your article. This phase of your work will include the following:

- Doing overview research
- Locating sources
- Outlining
- Writing first and subsequent drafts
- Editing your article for spelling, punctuation, grammar, and overall clarity and organization

Chapter 10 in this book will discuss research. Chapter 12 will discuss editing and revising.

7. Submit your article to the magazine that gave you the go-ahead.

As you work on researching and writing your article, you must keep this important point in mind: Make sure you are writing the article you told the editor in your query letter that you were going to write. The article you submit should be as close as possible in theme and plan to what you promised to the editor.

Make sure you have double- (and triple-) checked for any mistakes. The manuscript's appearance should be as neat as possible, there should be no mistakes, and it should be submitted professionally. Look back through the magazine's entry in *Writers Market*, or review its submission guidelines on its website or information sheet for writers, and be sure you submit in the way the editor expects.

You can submit your article manuscript through regular mail or by email — depending on what the editor wants.

8. Receive an acceptance from the magazine.

After submitting your manuscript, you will have to wait to get the final word from the magazine. With a go-ahead to a query, you can still receive a rejection — but you are less likely to have your article turned down if you have honored what you said in your query letter you would do and have submitted in a professional manner. You might receive a positive acceptance. In that case, the editor will give you details about publication of your article — when it will be published, how much you will be paid, and so forth.

9. Sign a contract.

Once you have received an acceptance, most magazines will have you sign a contract. The contract is important for a variety of reasons. It will let you know the following:

• What rights the magazine is purchasing. Most magazines purchase either *one-time rights*, which means you are giving up your rights to the article for the one time it is published in the magazine, or *all rights*, which means you are giving all your rights to the magazine and the article no longer belongs to you. It's probably already obvious to you that you should attempt to sell one-time rights, instead of all rights, whenever possible.

• How much you will get paid

• When your article will be published

• Other places where your article might be published (at the magazine's website, for example)

• Any information about the editing process. A statement such as "The magazine retains the rights to edit the submitted article as necessary, for editorial style, space, and other matters" may appear in the contract.

10. Get paid.

The payment for articles varies greatly in the magazine industry. A small, local magazine may pay you $50. A large, national magazine may pay you $1,500. Much of the disparity in payment comes from the huge variety in publications. Thousands of smaller magazines work on smaller budgets, while many high-circulation magazines have millions of dollars in advertising revenue.

Magazines pay in two different manners: on acceptance or on publication. If you are paid on acceptance, you will receive payment as soon as the editor accepts your article. If on publication, you will be paid when the article comes out in print.

As you begin your process as a freelance magazine writer, you can determine for yourself how much you would like to get paid for your writing. You can then be selective about where you submit your ideas. Realize, though, that there are dues to be paid and that it often takes awhile to build up to a larger income.

11. Receive a copy of your magazine and see your article in print.

You will receive one or more complementary copies of the magazine with your article in print. This is when you proudly show the magazine to everyone you know, or discreetly leave it on the coffee table in your den! Realize that magazines work with different lead times — the time it takes from acceptance to publication. So you might see your article in print within a month or so, but it may be a year down the road before you do.

12. Pitch another idea to the magazine.

You should follow up an acceptance with another pitch to that same magazine. By keeping your name in front of the editor, you're increasing your chances of regular publication. So, after you get an acceptance, always come up with another idea and send a query letter as soon as possible. Then, after your article comes out in print, contact the editor again with another idea or with a message that you're interested and open to article assignments.

13. And start all over with a new idea to other magazines.

The key to success as a freelancer is Perseverance (with a capital P!). You must stick with the process, always be thinking of article ideas, and have query letters out at all times. So, once you finish this process, start it all over again.

Use the *Writing Advantage* feature "Steps To Getting Published" on page 71 to keep track of the stages you go through as you attempt to get an article published.

What It Takes To Be a Successful Freelance Writer

Now that you understand the process, you will automatically find success in getting published, right?

That sounds nice, but now that you know the steps, you have to work hard at following the process. And, even then, some freelancers just seem to have more of a "magic touch" than others.

Why is that? What makes some writers more successful at getting published than others?

Successful and happy freelance writers share several traits. Here are the ones that characterize prolific writers:

Creativity

Successful writers are creative in the way they come up with article ideas, in how they incorporate writing into their larger life, in how they market themselves, and in how they develop a style for their writing. They are creative — they think outside of the box, if you will — in every aspect of their writing ambitions.

Specialization

They find an area for which they have an expertise. They discover they can specialize in it and develop articles for a variety of magazines. If they also have a passion for the subject, they find a great sense of purpose in writing about it.

Steps To Getting Published

Use the following list to keep track of the steps you need to take as you attempt to get published in magazines. Also use it as a checklist for each individual magazine article, to see what steps you have completed and what you still need to get done.

Check off each step once you complete it.

_____ 1. Develop a marketable idea

_____ 2. Do preliminary research

_____ 3. Locate possible magazine markets

_____ 4. Write and submit query letters

_____ 5. Receive a go-ahead

_____ 6. Research, write, and edit the article

_____ 7. Submit the article

_____ 8. Receive an acceptance

_____ 9. Sign a contract

_____ 10. Get paid

_____ 11. Receive a copy of the magazine with your article in it

_____ 12. Pitch another idea to that same editor

_____ 13. Start over with a new idea to a new magazine

Professionalism

They are focused on being the very best they can be in their writing. They value information, accuracy, and ethics. They approach editors with respect and attention to detail. They market and write in the most professional manner they can.

Passion

They love to write. They love being a writer. And they find something — travel, children, cooking, history, gardening, health, sports — that they can be passionate in writing about.

Persistence

They stick with the process and keep their goals in mind. That was true especially when they first started out as feature writers. They don't flinch when facing rejection. They believe in themselves and what they are trying to accomplish. They understand the wise Yoda (from the *Star Wars* movies) when he said, "Do or do not. There is no try." They give it everything they have.

Growth

They don't believe, however, that they are perfect or have already arrived at where they want to go. They know that they can always learn, always improve, always grow. They read about writing, attend writing conferences, take classes, network with other writers, keep up with the industry, study marketing trends — anything they can do to become a better writer than they are today.

As a freelance feature writer, you have the opportunity to develop your own ideas and choose what you write about. If you're not writing about something you enjoy, or people you're excited about, or things that pique your interest, then why are you writing?

Tackle your ideas, research, writing, and editing — all the parts of the article-writing process — with gusto. Take the enthusiasm you have for writing and channel it into every piece you write.

Readers sense passion. They know when you care about a topic. That, in turn, will create an invigorating symbiotic relationship between the reader and your work (and, in turn, you).

Exercises

1. Write down the names of any celebrity writers about whom you have read. Summarize what you learned about their writing life. Think about any writers you know personally. Write a paragraph about their writing life.

2. Write 300 words in response to the question "Why do I want to write?"

3. As you consider integrating writing into your life, consider your personality. In light of the characteristics mentioned in this chapter, what personality traits will help you to become a published writer? What traits will hinder you? How can you go about finding the success you desire?

4. As you look at the steps it takes to have an article published, make a chart listing the steps that you are confident in, have more questions about, and feel worried about trying.

Confident:	*Questions:*	*Worries:*
a.	a.	a.
b.	b.	b.
c.	c.	c.
d.	d.	d.
e.	e.	e.
f.	f.	f.
g.	g.	g.
h.	h.	h.

5. Make a list of five topics you could specialize in — topics you are especially suited to write about — and that you are especially passionate about.

Topic 1:

Topic 2:

Topic 3:

Topic 4:

Topic 5:

6. From one of the topics in Exercise 5, develop an idea for an article. Use the *Writing Advantage* feature "Steps To Getting Published" on page 71 to keep track of the article you'd like to write.

Generating Ideas for Articles

WHAT YOU WILL LEARN IN THIS CHAPTER

• Ideas are everywhere. Some of the best sources for ideas are what you know, what you'd like to know, other people, magazines' needs, things you read, the Internet, and the calendar.

• You can develop ideas with creative exercises.

• Not all ideas are publishable ideas. Spend time making sure your idea is one that you can research and write, that you will enjoy working on, and that is marketable.

Ideas for articles can come from almost anywhere.

I recently had an article on themed birthday parties — with a sidebar on fun and easy cupcake recipes — published in a number of regional parenting magazines. The article gave ideas for how parents can host creative, inexpensive birthday parties for children of different ages, and listed themes such as a princess party, scavenger hunt, and beach bash. This idea developed from years of planning and hosting parties for my three daughters. It came directly from my *personal experiences*.

Another recent article focused on a local community's effort to eradicate poverty and hunger by teaching the art of baking pies and, thus, build unity and fellowship among residents. I came upon this idea after reading about the program in a local newspaper. It came directly from my *reading*.

Several years ago, a history magazine published my article about Civil War photographer Mathew Brady. It focused on his interesting life and historical importance. It tied in with the 150th anniversary of his death. The idea came directly from this *anniversary aspect* of the topic.

A religious magazine recently published a personality profile of an author who writes teenage books from a Christian perspective. Her voice is something uncommon in today's young adult marketplace, and the idea came simply from thinking about my friends and acquaintances. It came from my *circle of relationships*.

To be a successful freelance writer, you must first develop good ideas for articles. Articles don't simply materialize out of thin air. Those great ideas submitted to editors must come from somewhere.

The question then is this: Where do marketable ideas come from?

The answer is simple: Anywhere and everywhere! Just look at the places the article ideas mentioned above came from. There are innumerable ideas waiting to be discovered. Writers just need to learn how to look for them.

Reader Needs

The first thing to realize in searching for publishable ideas is that all effective magazine articles fill some reader need. A feature writer's goal is to come up with ideas that will in some way help, entertain, inspire, or otherwise reach into the reader's life and needs. When you fill a reader's need, you are in turn filling an editor's need since an editor's main concern is the reader.

In thinking about readers of magazines, consider the following needs to which the professional writer consciously or unconsciously plays.

1. Readers want to be entertained, and reading is one of the ways they have fun. Their sources of entertainment can range over everything from traveling, to cooking, to sports, to hobbies, to pop culture.

2. Readers strive for emotional and physical health. They want to know how to make all aspects of their lives better.

3. Readers sometimes have problems with human relationships. Most problems relate to raising a happy family and maintaining nurturing relationships. Few things are higher on the list of concerns for most people than family and love.

4. Readers need help with their daily work. They want to do their work more quickly, easily, and productively.

5. Readers want to be well compensated for their work and be financially secure.

6. Readers want to be inspired by something bigger than themselves. They want to read stories of hope and courage. Such stories nourish their spirit.

In other words, readers want to be happy, healthy, loved, financially secure, and spiritually enriched. Editors are eager to get ideas that address any of these issues in a unique way.

Because of readers' needs, most magazines therefore emphasize *how-to* stories: (1) how to *do* something or (2) how to *be* something. Other types of articles — mentioned already in Chapter 5 — that fill such readers' needs include everything from personal experience pieces and travel articles to informational stories and short pieces. As long as a reader's need is being met, then the possibilities for article types, topics, and ideas are endless.

As you attempt to come up with ideas for articles that will fulfill readers' needs, you will be surprised by how many ideas you can develop ... *if* you are constantly aware that your daily life, activities, roles, memories, experiences, and relationships are the perfect fodder for ideas.

Let's consider some of the places you can find ideas for magazine articles.

Sources of Ideas #1: What You Know

You know the old adage that you should "Write what you know." It's an old adage for good reason. It's natural to write about the things you know about and feel comfortable with — whether it's a hobby you have, a place you visited, or a special expertise you possess. Let's break down your knowledge into three specific areas: personal experiences, personal interests and passions, and talents/areas of expertise.

Personal Experiences

Personal experiences are among the best sources for article ideas. For many writers, such experiences provide the source of most of their ideas. And it's natural that they do. When we have an experience we have learned from, or enjoyed, or have been inspired by, or that has simply made our life easier, we want to share it with other people. As writers, we find that our natural instinct is to sit down and write an article based on that experience.

As you look at the things you experience, consider two sources: the *mundane* things you experience on a daily basis and the *bigger* moments in your life. Both types of experiences can develop into marketable articles.

Ordinary moments — your commute to work, exercise regime, date night with your significant other — can become articles such as "De-Stressing Your Morning Commute," "Soccer for Grown-Ups," and "Fun Stay-at-Home Dates."

Bigger moments — the birth of a child, failure of a relationship, summer vacation — can become articles such as "10 Things I Wish I'd Known Before Having a Baby," "Be a Better Listener," and "Disney on a Budget."

Think back on your life and recall moments that were especially meaningful to you. They may be humorous moments (a fun vacation), significant moments (college graduation), emotional moments (birth of a child), life-changing moments (a divorce), sentimental moments (conversation with a grandmother), even small or seemingly routine moments (watching a sunrise).

These experiences — whether they taught you something, or entertained you, or changed you in some way — can develop into marketable articles. They might suggest an informative piece on how to handle a certain situation, a descriptive travelogue on a specific trip, or a personal essay on a memory from childhood.

Any time you write about something close to you, that intimacy in understanding and feeling will shine through.

Personal Interests and Passions

What are you particularly interested in? What hobbies or special activities do you engage in? What causes or topics are you particularly passionate about?

If you love something, it's a perfect subject to write about. After all, won't you be more passionate in your writing if you are passionate about the topic to begin with?

Think about the many things that personal interests and passions could encompass. Do you love photography, or wineries, or reality television? Do you crochet, or run marathons, or grow blueberries? Are you passionate about single-parent issues, or health care reform, or breast cancer?

Those interests and passions can easily develop into the types of articles that magazines need. Just think about the questions in the previous paragraph. Consider the following articles, among many, that could develop from your answers:

- "How to Take Your Own Holiday Portrait"
- "Little Known California Wineries"
- "Teaching Your Kids Through Reality Television"
- "A Crash Course in Crochet"
- "How to Eat for a Marathon"
- "Wild about Blueberry Pie"

- "When You and Your Teenager Both Date"
- "10 New Changes to Health Care Law"
- "Practical Ways to Help a Friend in Cancer Treatment"

Looking at all those possibilities, I think I might work on developing some of the ideas for myself!

Talents/Areas of Expertise

Another important area of "what you know" revolves around those things that you are good at — whether a physical talent or skill (such as running track or playing a musical instrument), psychological talent or skill (listening to and counseling others), or a professional area of expertise (teaching math or coaching softball).

The nature of feature writing is such that, once you have a byline in a publication, you are considered an expert. If you are a freelance writer, you are marketing yourself as an expert on a topic or issue. While you will back up your own areas of expertise with quotes and information from other expert sources, starting with something you are good at or know well is a fruitful way to begin.

All magazines — both general magazines and those that specialize in certain niches (such as hiking, teaching, music, or gardening) — need articles on specific skills, and they need skilled writers to write about those things.

Sources of Ideas #2: What You Don't Know ... Yet

While we usually lean toward writing about what we already know, there is something to be said for writing about things you don't know. Ideas developed from this perspective will stretch you creatively. You will come out of the process knowing much more than you did going in. And your curiosity about the topic should shine through in your writing.

Just because you aren't an expert on a topic doesn't mean you can't write about it. The questions to ask yourself are "What are some things I would like to know more about?" and "What would I love to read about them in a magazine?"

Let's break down "what you don't know" into three more specific areas: personal interests, personal dreams, and magazines' needs.

Personal Interests

What are some things you've always been interested in but don't know much about? Are there things you'd like to do or try? Are there things you enjoy but have never considered yourself able to write about?

For example, you may have an interest in environmental issues, even though you are not an expert on them. By doing research, talking to appropriate sources, and relying on your own curiosity, you can acquire the knowledge to write articles about the topic.

Don't be hesitant to contact sources. You might love watching science-fiction movies but would never consider trying to get in touch with producers or stars of those films. Why not? You might be surprised at whom you can interview and what articles you can sell.

Don't limit yourself just because you don't know much about the topic you're interested in.

Personal Dreams

Dreams and aspirations go further than personal interests. To generate ideas from them, ask yourself, "What dreams do I have? What are my goals? What do I want to accomplish? What do I really want to do with my life?"

One of my writing friends has a dream to travel. She yearns to go to Italy and experience the museums, wine, and pasta. She wants to visit Scotland and see the homestead of her ancestors. She hasn't been to either of those places — or many other ones she wants to visit someday — but she writes about them.

Another writer says that if she weren't a freelancer, she'd love to be either a baker or a sportscaster. While she didn't fulfill those professional dreams, she can still write about entertaining and sports — and she often does, much to her enjoyment.

In the grander scheme of things, people have many dreams and aspirations. Dreams of happy children. Dreams of spiritual purpose. Dreams of fulfillment in marriage and family and career.

Freelancers can write about those things.

Magazines' Needs

Another way to think about writing what you don't know is to approach article ideas from the back door. That is, instead of developing ideas based on your own interests or expertise, find out what specific magazines need. Then — whether you know about the topics or not — suggest articles on those topics to the magazines.

If, for example, you read a health magazine and see that its editors seem to especially like articles on healthy food choices and that they always include some sort of seasonal article, brainstorm ideas that fit into those areas — even if they aren't the sort of articles you would have come up with on your own.

Similarly, read through *Writer's Market* and get a sense of the types of articles specific magazines need. Then come up with some ideas — which may not have been the type you would have originally thought of — that fit the needs identified in the market guide. Browsing *Writer's Market* often will suggest many ideas to the imaginative freelancer.

Most magazines are predictable. They focus on specific topics, and many like to publish articles geared to specific issues throughout the year. The key for the freelancer is to come up with a new, fresh spin on those predictable topics. For example, if a magazine is interested in the topic "how to control your weight," a fresh spin for the November issue could be "how to control your weight during the holidays." The key is to think as the magazine's editor might think.

Sources of Ideas #3: Other People

You are not the only person who has valuable experiences, talents, areas of expertise, memories, hobbies, and dreams that could develop into magazine articles. Everyone has them.

Thus, other people can be sources for your feature article ideas. Their experiences and expertise are the perfect fields for you to dig around for topics and ideas that will interest readers. Well-known people, ordinary people who have done something extraordinary, people in the news, family, friends, associates, and other acquaintances, even strangers ... all can be good sources. Let's consider each group.

Well-Known People

Magazines love to get stories about celebrities or well-known people in certain fields (such as sports, technology, literature, or politics). So if you have connections to well-known people, you can probably find a market for your work. If you don't have such connections, often you can connect with celebrities in an easier fashion than you'd expect. They have agents and assistants who want to get them good press, and magazine articles are good ways to feature them.

I have done articles on several well-known sports figures and authors. Interviewing them usually has been an enjoyable experience — for they are more down-to-earth than you might expect — and they make for salable articles.

Ordinary People with Extraordinary Stories

Magazines are driven by readers — and readers love to identify with people like them who have an interesting story to tell. So magazines not only publish

Ginger Rue
"Writing for Teenagers"

Q: How did you get started writing for teenagers?

RUE: I was teaching middle school and high school English, and my students used a weekly reader magazine called *Writing!* It's no longer in print, but it was wonderful. It made writing instruction relevant to that age group, and so I asked the editor if I could write some articles for him. My first article was in that magazine and was about teen slang and how language evolves. Since then, I've written for *Seventeen*, *Sweet 16*, *Teen Vogue*, and many smaller teen magazines as well as national magazines for adults.

Q: Why did you find yourself attracted to writing for teenagers? What about that audience appealed to you?

RUE: I just think teenagers are tons of fun. I like explaining things to them, helping them with their issues. They are a lot smarter than people give them credit for, and they're interesting and often hilarious. If you care about them, they'll respond well to you most of the time. If you're condescending, they won't let you get away with it for long.

Q: Where do you come up with your article ideas?

RUE: I study the markets and see what kind of things they're looking for. Once you know that, you just keep your ear to the ground. When you find the right story, you know just where to pitch it.

Q: What were the greatest challenges you faced in getting published?

RUE: Not living in New York or having been on staff at a magazine. I've found that most freelance gigs are tossed to the editor's circle of acquaintances/colleagues, most of whom they know from having been on staff together at a magazine. It is possible to get in with a great pitch, but it's not easy. Once you do, work harder than anyone else so that when they

stories focusing on celebrities, but they also like stories about ordinary people who have found themselves in extraordinary situations.

Perhaps a person survived a traumatic ordeal, started a program to aid the poor, has an unusual hobby, did something one-of-a-kind, or won a national honor. These people are everywhere. You just have to be on the lookout for them and

need a story next time they'll call you because they know you'll make their life easier. Why shouldn't they give a freelance assignment to you instead of their roommate's boyfriend who needs to make his rent? Because they know you'll do a much better job, which will mean less time editing your work.

Q: What writing advice would you give aspiring writers/students?

RUE: Go the extra mile. If you have a deadline, don't miss it, or maybe turn in your assignment early. Make sure the editor doesn't mind, though. Some of them appreciate it, and others feel that getting something early messes up their schedule. Ask questions, but not ones you could find out for yourself if you'd just take the initiative to find out. Be organized. Give them everything they need for fact checking without having to ask for it.

Q: What marketing advice would you give?

RUE: Strive to be a dependable, pleasant person to work with. Word gets around, especially as editors move around to different magazines. A good reputation is the best form of marketing.

Q: What specific tips or ideas would you give writers especially interested in writing for teenagers?

RUE: Spend some time around teenagers! Don't try to be one of them, but observe how they talk and interact with each other. Ask them questions and listen to what they have to say. They'll probably be happy to talk to you if you treat them like they're interesting and important ... and they are!

Q: What are your future writing plans?

RUE: I hope to do the same thing I'm doing now: writing teen novels and doing magazine work. I love what I do!

Ginger Rue writes for various teenage magazines. She is also the author of two teenage novels — *Brand New Emily* and *Jump*.

---

recognize their story for what it can become for a magazine article.

Here are examples of articles about such ordinary people taken from real magazines:

- A man who survived a deadly tornado that ravaged the South. He lost his leg, but he would have died if not for the aid of strangers and neighbors.

- A quilter who had her work commissioned to appear in the White House
- A married couple who bought and restored an 1850 farmhouse
- A Wall Street analyst who spends her weekends at the mall, observing teenage fashion as a way of trying to predict trends
- A man who lost 40 pounds in one year through his own simple regimen of exercising and cutting out sweets
- A retiree who started a program to help farmers affected by injury or natural disaster

Those people had different experiences — but they were all "ordinary" people who had interesting experiences and unique stories to tell.

People in the News

Have you ever read about someone in your local newspaper, or seen someone on your local news, and thought to yourself, "Now, that person would make a great feature article"? What's keeping you from writing an article about that person? If the story was interesting enough for the local paper or television station, chances are that there would be plenty of other local, regional, or national markets for an article on the person.

You can also get article ideas from people you read or hear about in the news even though you don't intend to write an article solely about that person. If, for example, you read about a local youth soccer team coach who is particularly effective and inspiring to his players, you could use him as a source for an article on the importance of youth sports.

Family and Friends

I get countless ideas for articles based on my children — mostly because two of my writing specialties are children and family topics. The things they say, do, and experience all become inspiration for article ideas.

The same thing goes for all the people in your family. Think about your parents, siblings, grandparents, cousins, spouses, children, in-laws. What things about those people might inspire you with article ideas? For example, do you have a cousin who is a songwriter? Did your grandfather serve in World War II or Vietnam? Is your aunt a martial arts expert? Is your brother a veterinarian?

Acquaintances and Strangers

You don't have to write about only the people you know well. Always be on the lookout for an acquaintance, or a stranger you might meet in any situation.

One day I was standing in line at a local fast food restaurant when I met a woman — simply from striking up a conversation — who had decided to sell her house and all of her possessions in order to move to Israel and work as an English language teacher at a Christian school. Her story was fascinating, and I ended up writing an article about her for a religious publication.

Sources of Ideas #4: Things You Read

Freelancers' regular reading material — novels and nonfiction books, the Sunday newspaper, magazines, and favorite websites — often becomes fodder for article ideas.

Books

Both novels and nonfiction books can be inspirations for article ideas. Popular novels can give you an insight into what people like to read. Classic novels can inspire you with ideas that focus on classic themes. Nonfiction books can give you specific ideas for how-to and informational pieces.

One of the most popular nonfiction books in recent memory is *Midnight in the Garden of Good and Evil*, which is set in picturesque Savannah, Georgia. It inspired numerous magazine articles, including stories about Savannah sightseeing tours, other cities that are the settings of famous novels, a heavy metal band from Savannah, and the colonial history of Savannah — to name only a few. Published in 1994, the book still provides the inspiration for articles.

A book on the royal wedding of Prince William and Kate might give you an idea for a historical article on royal couples in the past, or one on how to find your own Prince Charming, or one on travel to royal British sites.

Also keep in mind that reference books — such as encyclopedias, books of days, and atlases — can be good sources as you brainstorm article ideas.

Newspapers

The daily newspaper should be one of your regular pieces of reading material. The lifestyle, sports, travel, and local sections are chock full of feature stories that can inspire article ideas.

Several years ago, I read about Tuscumbia, Alabama, in the "Day Trips" column of a newspaper's travel section. Tuscumbia was the home of Helen Keller. While just two hours away, I had never visited it. That changed. I toured the town and the Keller sites and subsequently had an article on the town published in a regional magazine.

A newspaper can give you specific ideas for articles — like the Keller story — and ideas for sources of information to use in articles.

It can also give you special insight into issues that are important to readers. In reading a newspaper, pay attention to things such as the economy, environment, and self-improvement. They are important. Also learn about which pop culture topics — such as celebrities, fashion, and music — are popular. Those insights can lead you to specific article ideas.

Magazines

Do you want to write for a particular type of magazine (such as children's, health, religious, gardening, or automobile) or a specific magazine (such as *Woman's Day, Atlanta Parent, Guideposts*, or *Sailing*)? One of the best ways to come up with article ideas is to read numerous issues of those publications you're interested in.

In reading a magazine, you will get insights into topics that it publishes. You can also take specific articles and come up with a new spin on them. For example, most women's magazines publish articles on topics such as fashion, beauty, relationships, self-improvement, and health. Think about those topics and the specific articles and then brainstorm for your own article ideas.

If you see an article in a teenage magazine titled "Don't Be a Victim of a Bully," think about how you could do a new spin on the topic. Perhaps you could query other teen magazines on articles such as "Are you a Bully?" or "How to Help a Friend Who Is Being Bullied," or "Learning To Be Comfortable in Your Own Skin." You could develop related article ideas for parenting magazines ("What If Your Child Is a Bully?") or educational magazines ("Spot Bullying Before It's a Problem in Your Classroom").

The Internet

Www are the three of the best letters ever invented for freelance writers. The Internet is a fertile place to do research, to find markets for publication, to help you come up with ideas for articles, and to be published.

The Internet changes daily and is a good gauge of the pulse of what's popular and meaningful to readers at the moment. Your daily read of news, celebrity, sports, parenting, health, and food websites will give you countless ideas for articles every day.

The next time you surf simply for entertainment or distraction, take a closer look at what you're reading. What topics could you develop into article ideas?

Other Reading Material

Think about all the things you read that are atypical — things like that college pamphlet, advertisements, catalogs, telephone directories, billboards. Any reading material can be a source for ideas.

For example, my oldest daughter recently went off to college several hours from our home. As I tried to prepare for her living away from home and aspired to be the "right" sort of college parent, I studied the freshman parenting guides the university provided as a resource. As the beginning of the school year rolled around, I sold an article titled "A Parent's Freshman Year Survival Guide" to two magazines.

Sources of Ideas #5: Seasons, Holidays, and Anniversaries

Magazines are cyclical creatures — they are published every month, bi-monthly, quarterly, sometimes even weekly. So they're always alert for topics that are going to be important to readers at certain times of the year.

As you try to come up with article ideas, think about ones that would be timely in connection with the following:

- Winter, spring, summer, or fall issues
- Specific months
- Certain holidays — the "big" ones like Christmas, Thanksgiving, and Easter, but also the "smaller" ones like President's Day, St. Patrick's Day, Mother's Day, and Constitution Day

It's easy to plan many ideas for the entire year simply by thinking ahead. To do that, start the new year by writing down the months in a notebook and then brainstorming specific ideas that fit each month. Think of issues that are important for every month, as well as the holidays during the month. A calendar that lists holidays will prove helpful.

Magazines also publish anniversary pieces on a regular basis. These are stories that celebrate the 5th, 10th, 25th, 50th, 100th ... or any other milestone ... anniversary of an event. Such articles can fit neatly in historical magazines, but they also work for niche magazines (such as, for example, retirement, religious, and farm publications). Think of such things as the anniversary of technological advances (the personal computer), momentous events (9-11), births and deaths of influential people, and so forth. A book that lists historical events day by day, year by year, can be a valuable tool as you look for anniversary topics.

Sources of Ideas #6: Evergreen Topics

Certain topics are "evergreen" — meaning they are popular every year on a repetitive basis. Every January, for example, magazines publish articles on New Year's resolutions and winter health. August issues have articles on back-to-school topics and summer-heat issues. December issues focus on decorating for Christmas, gift ideas, cooking Christmas cookies, Hanukkah traditions, and similar topics.

Magazines also publish on certain topics that are always popular with readers. Women's magazines publish evergreen articles on fashion, health, relationships, self-improvement, beauty, and other niche topics. Food magazines publish articles on recipes, cooking techniques, chefs, and health.

Put yourself in the mind of a typical reader — and brainstorm. What article ideas can you think of that appeal to you during a year's cycle? What topics do you want to read about regularly?

Sources of Ideas #7: Creative Exercises

We all have times when our creative juices run a little dry and we can't think of any new ideas. We can sit all day and think about our recent experiences, read a month's worth of newspapers, and talk to people we know ... and we still can't think of any ideas. We also have those times when we just need to shake things up a little bit and stretch our imagination. We need to find a new way to expand our creativity.

It's in these dry times that you might want to turn to creative exercises to develop story ideas. These exercises are fun, imagination-stretching ways to come up with story ideas in a random, brainstorming way.

Following are some creative exercises that you can use successfully to generate ideas.

Idea Chart

I can thank my favorite college professor for this imaginative idea, which is guaranteed to provide you 25 article ideas in a matter of minutes.

Create a page with six columns running down it and six rows running across, giving you a total of 36 boxes. Leave the top left box blank. Then, in each of the remaining five boxes across the top of the page, write down five different types of magazines (such as women's, teen, sports, music, and retirement) that you'd like to write for. In each of the remaining five boxes down the left side of the

Idea Chart

List a general subject in each box below	List a category of magazine in each box across this top row				

page, write down five different topics (such as flowers, hip hop, history, photography, and marathons) that you'd like to write about.

The *Writing Advantage* feature on this page shows how the Idea Chart is set up.

In each box — where a topic row and a magazine column intersect (say, flowers and retirement magazines) — develop a story idea that fits the two together (that is, an idea about flowers for a retirement magazine, perhaps "Gardening with Your Grandchildren"). This approach will result in your having ideas slanted toward specific types of magazines. Because of the distinctive way the box fits ideas to magazines, the ideas you create may be ones with a slant that no other freelancer has thought of.

"I love" ("I hate," "I wish," etc.)

At the top of a blank page of paper, write the term "I love" and then write a list of all the things you can think of that you love. Big or small, politics or choco-

Five Exercises
To Get the Juices Flowing

Sometimes writers feel as if their brain has just gone dead, and they struggle to come up with anything that seems interesting. They need a break to get a fresh view. If that happens to you, try these creative exercises the next time you need an article idea.

1. Editor for an Hour
Pick up a favorite magazine, read through its pages, and imagine that you are its editor. Make a list of at least 10 articles you'd print in your magazine.

2. Music Appreciation
Turn the radio on to your favorite station, turn on your favorite CD, or select some music that you've never heard before. Let your mind take you in a creative direction. What does the music remind you of? What words does it make you think of? What type of person would enjoy this music? Jot down any article ideas you immediately think of.

3. Day at the Coffee Shop
Spend an afternoon at a local coffee shop (or library, or shopping mall, or any public place), and jot down any particular observations you make. What article ideas come to you?

4. Newspaper Search
Read the latest Sunday edition of your local newspaper (or read it online). Look through its pages, noticing in particular the topics, events, people, and issues that could apply well to a regional or national magazine.

5. A Look at the Calendar
Start with today's date. Then look at the calendar and jot down the date it will be in six months. Based on that future date, come up with a list of seasonal or holiday article ideas. Then do the same thing with the date one year from today.

---

late chip cookies — it doesn't matter. Give yourself four or five minutes, brainstorming as quickly as you can, to come up with a full page. Then think about specific article ideas you can develop from the items you wrote down. If you love something, chances are you can write about it.

Do the same exercise with "I hate" or "I wish" — or any other short introductory phrase that captures your feelings about things.

Photographic Memory

Gather together some of your photo albums or loose photographs you have from a certain event (a trip or a wedding, for example) or from the past (your childhood or college years, for example). Then let your mind wander to the memories of those moments. What made the moments special? What specific things do you remember? Would you want to do them again? If you're in the photos, what were you thinking about when each picture was taken?

You know that your experiences are great fodder for article ideas. Bringing up images from the past can help produce some of those ideas.

Other creative exercises can work just as well in generating ideas. Check out the *Writing Advantage* feature "Five Exercises To Get the Juices Flowing" on page 90 for more quick ideas to try the next time you need a fresh approach to finding ideas. You can also find exercises by searching online.

See the *Writing Advantage* feature "Ideas Generated from a Day of Brainstorming" on page 92 for an example of article ideas developed in a typical session.

Slanting Your Article Ideas

Perhaps the most distinctive aspect of ideas for magazine articles is *slanting*. It is of critical importance. It is not a concept one often encounters outside magazines. To become successful at publishing feature articles, though, freelancers must understand slanting and how to do it.

The reason slanting is so important is that all magazines target specific audiences. Some magazines, for example, are aimed at readers interested in sports, others are aimed at readers interested in gardening, others are aimed at readers interested in personal computers, and a few are even aimed at a general audience.

Look, for example, at the table of contents in *Writer's Market*, and you will see more than 100 categories of interests of consumer and trade magazines. The categories range from "animal" to "women's" and from "advertising" to "veterinary." Each category indicates the reader interest at which magazines in the category are aiming.

Then, among magazines in the same category one will find even more specific targeting. In the "photography" category, for example, *Nature Photographer*

Ideas Generated from a Day of Brainstorming

Sometimes you should set aside a time simply to try to generate ideas for articles. Here's an example. It was at the end of June, our family had just returned from vacation, my daughters were out of school, I had recently attended a wedding, I watched baseball, and I looked forward to the end of summer. The following ideas came from a short session of thinking of article possibilities:

"Writing During the Summer"
"Setting and Meeting Goals"
"Raising Patriotic Kids"
"Host a Fourth of July Block Party"
"Fun Trivia about Our Founding Fathers"
"The Best Hidden Beaches on the Gulf"
"How To Make Better-than-Restaurant Gumbo"
"Be a Productive Vacation Packer (and Un-Packer)"
"20 Ways To Keep Learning Over the Summer"
"10 Fun Stay-cations"
"Wedding Etiquette 101"
"Fairy Tale Romances Still Happen Today"
"Fun Wedding Reception Ideas"
"Girls Love Baseball, Too!"
"The Value of Youth Sports"
"Tips for Saving Money on College Tuition"
"Raising a Reluctant Student"

"emphasizes nature photography that uses low-impact and local less-known locations, techniques, and ethics." *PC Photo*, on the other hand, "is designed to help photographers better use digital technologies to improve their photography." A third magazine, *Photo Techniques*, covers "photochemistry, lighting, optics, processing, printing, Zone System, digital imaging/scanning/printing, special effects, sensitometry, etc."

Every magazine will have its particular emphasis. That emphasis is its *slant*. Each magazine publishes only articles that fit its slant. That means that, to be successful, freelancers must slant their ideas to each magazine's particular interest. If a writer proposes an article without an appropriate slant, the magazine editor is almost certain to reject it.

You can get an idea of how topics can be slanted to different magazines by looking again at the "Idea Chart" on page 89 in this chapter. For each subject that you listed in the left column, when you came up with an idea about it for a specific type of magazine, you were providing a new slant on the subject.

Not only are understanding and practicing slanting critical for a freelancer's publishing success, but a writer who masters the process will find success multiplied. To begin with, the writer will know how to make an idea appeal to a specific magazine. Then the writer can take the same idea, tweak it by taking another angle on it, and make it appropriate for a second magazine. More angles will make the idea fit more magazines. With slanting, you can take *one* general idea and develop it into *many* possible articles.

To be productive as a freelancer, you should try to maximize publications from your ideas so that you are selling as many articles as possible on each idea. The best way to maximize the number of articles that you get published is to think of as many slants as possible to every idea you develop.

As an example of slanting, imagine that a writer has an idea for a travel article on the best zoos in the United States. While his first thought may be simply to write a general, overview article on the the country's best zoos, that specific approach alone will limit the marketing possibilities. By slanting the idea and coming up with different angles, the writer can maximum the number of articles he might get published. He could slant his idea more specifically and come up with these other ideas:

1. The best zoos in a particular part of the country (the South, the Midwest, a specific state, etc.), marketed to regional or city magazines

2. Going on a "zoo tour" with your kids as a summer road trip, marketed to parenting magazines

3. The best zoos in overseas countries, for travel magazines

4. One particular zoo's special event (perhaps a Christmas "safari party"), with a sidebar on other zoos in the country that do similar events, marketed for general-interest or travel magazines

5. The most educational zoos and programs, marketed to education or home-schooling magazines

The writer could develop any other number of articles based on zoo-related topics, such as having parties at zoos, the most popular current exhibits at zoos, profiles of particular zoos or zoo directors, and on and on.

To experiment with how many targeted ideas you can develop from one general idea, try this game: Think of a general subject, such as "music," look through the categories of magazines listed in *Writer's Market,* and give a slant to your subject that makes it appropriate for as many magazine categories as you can.

To slant one idea into two, three, or many more article ideas, you should consider these questions:

1. What are the different aspects to the topic that might be interesting to a reader?

2. Who are the different audiences who might be interested in this idea or topic?

3. What different types of magazines (or what specific magazines) might be interested in different angles to this idea?

Coming up with different slants on one idea is of great value for feature writers. It gets the most results out of the research and writing process. Although the different slants will result in different articles, the same research and some of the same writing can be used in the different articles. Slanting thus makes the most of a writer's time and energy. Whenever you come up with an idea for a feature article, always go to the next level and ask yourself: "How can I slant this idea in a different way and sell *another* article based on it?"

Do You Have a *Good* Idea?

You are now equipped with numerous ways to come up with ideas. And, if you're serious about getting your articles published, you'll come up with plenty of them.

Just because you can come up with ideas, though, doesn't mean that all of them are good ones. In fact, most of the ideas a writer generates probably don't develop into ideas that are publishable. You'll probably discard many ideas that might at first seem interesting to you. Don't waste time researching and writing queries on an idea that probably is not publishable.

Ideas don't develop into published stories for many reasons. Perhaps there's no market for them. Or the writer can't practically do the research to write the articles. Or, after thinking about the idea, the writer senses that it doesn't "feel" right.

Ask the following questions about each of your article ideas. They can help you determine whether it is usable or can develop into a publishable article.

1. Is the subject interesting for readers of the publication?

2. Is it sufficiently helpful to readers?

3. Is it narrow enough, or is it too general?

4. How important is it?

5. How many people will it entertain or interest? Does it have wide appeal?

6. How many times has the idea been used? Has it been overdone?

7. Does the subject excite *you*?

8. Are you truly able to research, write, and complete the article?

9. Can you find more than one potential market for the idea?

Keep Track of Your Ideas

It is amazing how many ideas a writer can come up with in the span of one day — or even an hour or two. It is also amazing how many ideas one can forget if not using a means to keep track of them.

While you're engaged in the idea-generating process, make sure you keep track of your ideas in a practical, manageable way so that you don't forget them.

Here are some ways that will help you keep up with your ideas.

1. *Jot down ideas in notebooks.*

Keep a small notebook around you all the time — in your pocket or purse, in your car (just in case you forget to put your notebook in your pocket), and on your bedside table. With your notebook at hand, you are able to write down ideas as soon as you think of them. If you don't write them down immediately, you could easily forget them.

2. *Keep an idea log.*

Keep track of the ideas you come up with and what you do with them. You must have a way to remember if the idea is simply an idea — or if you've researched it, submitted it to a magazine, or saved it for a later day. See the *Writing Advantage* feature "Idea Log" on page 96 for an example of how to keep track of your ideas.

3. *Keep everything organized on a computer.*

Everyone has a different way of keeping records. Some writers keep everything in hard-copy folders. However, because of the convenience of the computer, some writers use it exclusively to keep track of article ideas. Set up folders and sub-folders on your computer to keep track of ideas — and then of your articles as they develop.

Idea Log

Keep track of your ideas with this easy-to-use log. Write down your ideas and what you do with them: what magazines you query, when you send them out to a magazine, and any response you get.

Article Idea	Magazine Queried	Date Queried	Response Received
1.			
2.			
3.			
4.			
5.			
6.			
7.			
8.			
9.			
10.			

What Do You Do Next?

Finding an idea is just the beginning of the process. You still have to find potential markets for the idea, write query letters, research and write your article, and submit the manuscript.

The following chapters in this book will fill in the blanks of the steps in the process.

Exercises

1. Complete the "Idea Chart" on page 89 in this chapter. If you run out of space for all the ideas you generate, make copies of the chart and continue to fill in the boxes for ideas.

2. Spend a day generating ideas. Be in a creative state of mind all day long, and write your ideas down in your journal or in the space below.

3. Come up with five article ideas based on your personal experiences.

    a.

    b.

    c.

    d.

    e.

4. Come up with five ideas from people you know.

    a.

    b.

    c.

    d.

    e.

5. Come up with five ideas from things you have read recently.

    a.

    b.

    c.

    d.

    e.

6. Come up with five ideas based on your areas of expertise.

    a.

    b.

    c.

    d.

    e.

7. Come up with five ideas based on your hobbies and interests.

    a.

    b.

    c.

    d.

    e.

8. Come up with five ideas based on things you'd like to know more about.

    a.

    b.

    c.

    d.

    e.

Marketing Your Writing

- Marketing one's writing is essential for success as a feature writer.

- The writer must keep up-to-date with potential markets for article ideas.

- Social networking and online tools are essential in marketing.

- Articles can be marketed with different slants, resulting in multiple sales.

One writer comes up with great ideas for articles and then crafts interesting, well-written articles from them. Her list of credits now numbers more than a hundred.

A second writer comes up with just as many great ideas, but they remain in her folder of ideas. They don't actually develop into published articles. She is still waiting for that first published credit.

While being a good writer is important, it is *not* the hallmark of the person who gets published most often. Sometimes, in fact, the best writers never get published.

Why are some writers successful and others not?

The main reason is that some understand marketing and others don't. Marketing is a vital skill in getting published in magazines — and other markets, as well — but not everyone knows how to do it. Successful writers understand the industry, can find markets for their work, know how to query an editor, and develop good relationships with editors.

Marketing skills can be mastered. An aspiring feature writer can learn them all, greatly improving his chances of getting published from the very start.

Keeping Current with Markets

The most basic thing — the first thing — to do to market articles successfully is to keep current with magazines and other markets that accept freelance material.

Anyone who succeeds as an expert in any field, or who does something well, keeps up-to-date with what's going on in the industry. The best real estate agent knows all about housing, buyer, and seller trends. The best teacher knows all about current teaching philosophies and methods. And the best, most successful (i.e., published) feature writers know what's going on in the publishing industry.

To keep current with markets, a feature writer must do the following:

1. Read magazines regularly.

Know what magazines are popular. Know which ones are new. Know which ones are going out of business. Know what readers seem to enjoy reading.

2. Stay informed about industry news.

Many magazines, newspapers, and websites publish information about the publishing industry. Reading them will give you the "inside" track on what's going on with magazines and other markets for your freelance work. One of the best places to read this information is *Writer's Digest Magazine.* It includes a monthly marketing column that lists such things as new magazines and the particular freelance needs of specific magazines. Websites about the publishing industry and periodicals such as *Folio Magazine* and *The Writer* can be especially helpful.

Finding Markets

The previous chapter should have provided you with plenty of ideas. After you have developed an idea for an article, the next step is to find a magazine or other market that might be interested in it. This job is, for many people, the hardest part of the writing/publishing process. They can come up with ideas and know exactly how they're going to craft the article, but they can't find a good place to submit their idea.

As with so many things covered in this book, the key is to know the proper procedure. Literally tens of thousands of publications exist. Finding the right one for a feature idea simply involves a dedication to the process. You just need to know how to find the magazines that will want to publish your article.

Several important sources of marketing information about specific magazines are geared specifically to freelancer writers — the *Writer's Market* guide, magazines' writing guidelines, magazine websites, and magazines themselves.

Writer's Market

Using *Writer's Market* is the vital, necessary step to market articles. The guide is integral to every magazine writer's life.

Writer's Market is published annually by Writer's Digest Books and includes up-to-date information on all the possible markets for your writing, whether it is for magazine articles, books, short stories, novels, plays, scripts, greeting cards, or fillers. The magazine article category is the largest one listed in the book.

Each year the book is updated so that all information about publishers is current. Most editions include an addition of several hundred new magazine markets, and all the information about markets — even the same magazines that are listed each year — is updated by 85% over the previous year's book. The guide is especially important to feature writers, because it keeps them up-to-date on current markets and, more importantly, gives detailed information on how to submit articles to specific magazines.

Writer's Market divides magazines into a number of categories (for example: children's, hobby, travel, and women's magazines). Within each category is a list of specific magazines and the individual details and requirements of each one — such as the magazine's circulation, staff, editorial needs, payment, and other topics that will aid freelance writers.

How do you use *Writer's Market* to find a specific magazine for an article idea? Here are the steps:

1. Determine who the audience for your idea might be. In other words, who would want to read your article?

2. Once you know your audience — for example, runners, businessmen, senior citizens, women, college students, etc. — think about what types of magazines those people read.

3. Read the Table of Contents in *Writer's Market* and determine which magazine categories fit your idea. You might decide, for example, that camping, regional, and travel magazines are the most appropriate ones.

4. Look up specific magazines in each of the categories and read their entries.

5. Based on that information, select the magazines that your idea appears to fit best.

As an example, let's imagine you have come up with an idea for an article tentatively titled "The Country's Best Zoos," which you want to be a roundup piece about the top 10 zoos to visit in the United States. Following the steps listed above, here is how you would identify markets for your idea:

1. Determine several different audiences, which might include travelers, retired individuals, animal lovers, children, and parents.

2. Based on those potential readers, decide to slant the idea and market it to a number of different types of magazines. Potential markets could include travel magazines, retirement magazines, RV magazines, animal magazines, pet magazines, children's magazines, parenting magazines, and any others you consider appropriate.

3. Read the Table of Contents in *Writer's Market*. You find that it includes these categories: Animal, Child Care & Parental Guidance, General Interest, Juvenile, Retirement, Camping, and Travel.

4. Look up those categories in *Writer's Market* and identify specific magazine markets for the article idea, especially ones that take travel pieces, such as *Family Fun, Kids Life, American Profile, Grit, Open Spaces, Cricket, U.S. Kids, Mature Years, AAA Going Places, Family Motor Coaching*, and *Motorhome*.

5. Examine the entry for each magazine to determine specifically what the editor wants to receive from freelance writers. If a magazine appears to be interested in the type of idea you have in mind, complete the process by slanting your idea in a way to make it appropriate for the magazine. Then submit a query about your idea to the editor.

The process takes some research and time, but this simple plan to use *Writer's Market* analytically will pay dividends by identifying a number of magazines to submit to.

To understand what the guide offers to freelancers, consider this typical entry in *Writer's Market*:

$$$ Better Nutrition

Active Interest Media, 300 N. Continental Blvd., Suite 650, El Segundo CA 90245. Phone: (310) 356-4100. Fax: (310) 356-4110. E-mail: editorial@betternutrition.com.

Website: www.betternutrition.com. Contact: Tracy Rubert, mng. ed. 57% freelance written. Monthly magazine covering nutritional news and approaches to optimal health. "The new Better Nutrition helps people (men, women, families, old, and young) integrate nutritious food, the latest and most effective dietary supplements, and exercise/personal care into healthy lifestyles." Estab. 1938. Circ. 460,000. Byline given. Pays on publication. No kill fee. Publishes ms an average of 2 months after acceptance. Rights purchased varies according to article. Editorial lead time 3 months. Accepts queries by mail, email. Sample copy free.

Nonfiction: Each issue has multiple features, clinical research crystallized into accessible articles on nutrition, health, alternative medicine, disease prevention. Buys 120-180 mss/year. Query. Length: 400-1200 words. Pays $400-$1000.

Photos: State availability of photos. Captions, identification of subjects, model releases required. Reviews 4 x 5 transparencies, 3 x 5 prints. Negotiates payment individually. Buys one-time rights or non-exclusive reprint rights.

Tips: "Be on top of what's newsbreaking in nutrition and supplementation. Interview experts. Fact-check, fact-check, fact-check. Send in a resumé (including IRS number), a couple of clips, and a list of article possibilities."

You can see that the entries in *Writer's Market* provide many items of importance, including the following:

1. Contact information (address, phone number, email address) of the publication

2. Information about editors and to whom articles/query letters should be addressed

The type of editor varies from publication to publication. The contact person may be a managing editor, an articles editor, or even a specific department editor.

3. Information about how much freelance material is used

This information is especially helpful in determining which magazines are open to freelance writers.

4. Circulation information

Smaller magazines are often the best publications for the beginning freelancer to approach. Big magazines usually pay more for articles, and so they attract experienced writers and more queries.

5. Subject matter and word length for articles

6. Publication and contract information

These details will cover such matters as how much a magazine pays, what rights to your article it buys, and when it responds to your query letter.

7. Editorial needs and topics of interest

This information is *very* important as you initially try to determine if the magazine fits your idea. If, for example, your article is a how-to piece and the magazine doesn't list how-to articles as a need, don't waste time proposing the idea to that magazine.

8. Specific tips the editor finds important

When submitting a query letter, use the entry information from *Writer's Market* as a specific guide. Follow a magazine's guidelines as closely as possible. Adhering to the guidelines shows the editor that you have done the important research into the magazine's needs and that you know what you're doing. For example, if a magazine's entry says it accepts articles in the 800-1,000 word length range, don't submit an idea for a 1500 word article. If it says it only accepts travel essays, don't submit an idea for a personal profile.

See the *Writing Advantage* feature "Determining the Right Magazine for Your Idea" on page 105 to help determine a list of possible markets for your specific ideas.

Writers' Guidelines

The entry in *Writer's Market* gives you all the basic information you need to know about a magazine — and it's all you'd need to know to write a good query letter. If you want more specific information, though, it's worth getting writing guidelines from the magazine. See the *Writing Advantage* feature "Sample Writing Guidelines" on page 106 for an example of writers' guidelines.

Magazines provide writing guidelines as a handy way for freelancers to learn about the publications' needs and wants. The guidelines will give information similar to that found in *Writer's Market* (contact information, editorial needs, payment information, rights policies, etc.), but the following two pieces of information can be found only in guidelines.

1. An editorial calendar

Most magazines have a specific schedule for at least a year ahead of time, and editors plan articles according to this schedule. Many magazines will promote their editorial calendar in their writing guidelines, letting potential writers know what article ideas might work especially well for specific months. An editorial calendar will say, for example, that its July issue will include an article on patriotic desserts, lake safety, and skin cancer prevention.

Determining the Right Magazine for Your Idea

You've got an idea for an article that you think could be really great. You're not sure, though, of the right market for it. Use the following worksheet any time you are trying to find a suitable market for an article idea. It should help you develop several possible markets for the story.

1. My idea:

2. Audiences who might be interested in this topic (for example, women, travelers, cooks, and crafters):

3. Categories of magazines (for example, women's, juvenile, general interest, and regional) these audiences read:

4. Type of article into which this idea might develop (for example, how-to, narrative, or profile):

5. A possible target magazine for this article and additional information I need to know about it (for example, word limits and editor's tips, etc.):

6. Another possible magazine and additional information:

7. Another possible magazine and additional information:

---

2. A theme list

Some magazines go into even more depth and focus on specific themes for each issue. The writing guidelines will reveal these themes sometimes two or three years in advance — which makes the theme list especially effective as a means for freelancers to come up with marketable article ideas. Parenting magazines, for example, list such themes as Summer Camp, Holiday Travel, and Back-to-school. A children's history magazine is much more specific, listing such topical issues as Mayan Culture, History of the Circus, and Early American Inventors.

Magazine Websites

The Internet has made it much easier for freelancers to gain important mar-

Sample Writing Guidelines

Bride & Groom Magazine

We accept queries and complete articles from freelance writers on any and all topics relating to wedding planning and trends. Please keep in mind that we angle our articles to fit our regional audience and, therefore, must pre-approve all sources. We suggest that you read a few issues to get a sense of our style and presentation. Unsolicited articles and queries (see guidelines below) — accompanied by clips and a resumé — may be sent by e-mail to the editor (please put "Article Query" in the subject line), or by regular mail (non-returnable) to Bride & Groom Magazine, Attn: Managing Editor, 334 Boston Turnpike, Shrewsbury, MA 01545. We are not responsible for any original material submitted by regular mail.

What We Accept
• Regular articles on a particular topic with two - three sources quoted (minimum word count 750).
• Feature articles covering major topics such as reception sites, event planning, the latest wedding trends, etc., that highlight three to five sources and are run with professional photos (minimum word count 1200).
• Honeymoon articles featuring either one or more sites/destinations (minimum word count 750). A list of PR contacts (and their contact information) is required.

Writer's Guidelines
• Manuscripts submitted electronically should be as MSWord documents using the Times or Times New Roman font in 10-pt. or 12-pt. and single-spaced.
• When quoting local resources, include full contact name, business name, and the city and state in which they are based.
• Sidebars are welcome and encouraged.
• Professional photos illustrating the topic covered in your article are also welcome. Image files should be .jpg or .tif with a minimum resolution of 300 dpi and a minimum dimension of 4" x 6". Please include detailed captions and the proper photo credit (listing the photographer's name and including a Web address or phone number). Multiple images should be sent on a CD. Single images under 8MB may be e-mailed to the editor.
• Pay rate is a flat fee determined by the type of article written and is discussed directly with the writer.

keting information about publications. Most magazines have either online versions of their print editions or informational websites that include information about their print versions, sometimes including archives of some articles. Both types of websites invariably include information about the editorial staff, editorial needs, and submission policies. Many have the magazines' full writing guidelines, including the same information provided in their printed guidelines.

When looking at a magazine's website, find a place on the menu that refers to "Editorial Guidelines" or something similar. If there is nothing that obvious, go to the "About Us" or "Contact Us" button. These buttons often will link to the magazine's writing guidelines.

Many other websites provide lists and databases of freelance magazine markets. The sites are similar to *Writer's Market*, but they compile the information in a free, even more accessible manner. Some excellent ones are the following:

www.writingfordollars.com
www.writing-world.com
www.writersdigest.com
www.writersmarket.com
www.writing.com
www.bellaonline.com
www.newsu.com
www.gigsforwriters.com
www.fundsforwriters.com
www.mediabistro.com

Magazines

Although it's been mentioned before, it's worth repeating: As an aspiring feature writer, you should have magazines as one of your main interests. You should enjoy reading them and scanning magazine racks in bookstores. You should know how to study a magazine from cover to cover. You should be familiar enough with the field that you know when a new magazine appears or when one goes out of business.

If you have an idea for an article, you can go to the magazine section of a library or bookstore and find several possible markets. If you are an avid reader, you will know if magazines have recently published articles on the topic you're interested in writing about.

Once you decide on a specific magazine for which you want to write, obtain several copies of the magazine and study them. In particular, notice the follow-

Dan Case
"Making Money as a Feature Writer"

Q: What is your background? Were you a freelancer or editor and then decided to start your website?

CASE: I've been writing magazine articles since 1981. In 1997, when I needed to create a website that would use a database (for learning how to program on the Internet), I naturally chose to do a database of magazine writers' guidelines.

Q: What does your website provide for freelancers?

CASE: I started with a free database of writers' guidelines on our AWOC website (www.awoc.com) and started a monthly newsletter (now weekly) called "Writing for DOLLARS." The newsletter became so popular that I moved the database and newsletter to its own website, writingfordollars.com, in 1999. We've published nearly 600 articles on the business of writing since 1997, and all of the articles are archived on our website for free.

We also started publishing books for writers in 2000 with the publication of *The Complete Guide to Writing and Selling Magazine Articles* by Peggy Fielding and myself. We've since branched out into other genres.

---

ing details:

1. The types of topics the magazine covers
2. Specific articles it has published in the last year
3. Particular interests the editor has
4. The use of freelance writers, as compared to staff writers. Compare bylines with the list of staff members.
5. The structure of the articles and the writing style they use

Other Writers

One of the best ways to find out about possible markets is to network with other freelancers. Writers can share with each other about magazines that are looking for material, specific editors and what they like, and other important information about publication possibilities.

Over the years, I have been involved with several writing conferences where I have networked with hundreds of fellow writers. I have also been a part of local

Q: In regard to making money at freelancing, what are some of the important marketing tips/tactics that writers need to keep in mind?

CASE: The first and foremost thing is to write something good ... duh. Sounds like a given, but you wouldn't believe the number of wannabe writers who turn out crappola and wonder why they can't sell it.

Learning your craft is the most important thing any writer can do. And that takes lots and lots of practice. Have you ever heard anyone say, "Write every day"? Believe it: it's true. Once you can turn out a good article, book, play, whatever ... the marketing is actually the easy part.

Q: What advice do you wish you had been told when you were starting out as a writer (and that you would give to aspiring writers today)?

CASE: I was very fortunate in learning from the best. So there were no surprises for me. So that is my advice. Listen to successful writers. Ignore those who haven't sold a thing.

Dan Case is the owner of the popular writing website www.WritingforDollars.com. It is an invaluable guide for freelancers that includes such resources as a weekly newsletter, archive of articles on writing topics, and an extensive database of magazine markets.

---

writing groups, where I have learned valuable information about local and regional publishing opportunities — and have made good friends and found a supportive circle of relationships.

To find a local writing group, call local libraries and chambers of commerce. Do a Web search for writing groups in your area. If there's not one, why not start one of your own?

When she couldn't find a local group, writer Cindy Jones started one. She found a local church that would let the group meet in its facilities. Then she began promoting the group with an easy-to-set-up blog and website, on Facebook, and with flyers in her area. "Another writer and I wanted a place where we could gather with like-minded people to talk, learn, and encourage each other," Jones said. "The group meets once a month and uses a mixture of hands-on writing time, workshops, guest speakers, and group discussions."

Writing conferences — most of which are held during the summer — provide writers with opportunities to talk with other writers, attend workshops, learn from prolific and published writers, and network with publishers and editors. To find a writing conference or workshop to attend, Google "writing conferences" or check out the listings at www.writersdigest.com.

Social Networking and Technology-Friendly Marketing

With the world at our fingertips via the Internet, countless opportunities exist to market your writing. Along with using websites and web searches to locate markets for article ideas, writers can also use the Internet to market themselves to editors/magazines using a variety of social networking and web-based techniques.

Consider the following marketing ideas.

Personal Websites and Blogs

Setting up a personal website is a great way to market your freelance writing. You can share information about yourself and provide links to your published writing that can be found on other websites and magazine pages. Depending on your creativity, tech savvy, and energy, you can make your website as sophisticated as you want. It doesn't have to be elaborate, though, to be effective. A simple website can be effective if you provide good information on it.

Once you have a website to promote yourself and your writing, list it on everything you own! Use it in your signature line or contact information line on queries and e-queries you send out. Put it on business cards. Let all your acquaintances know about it.

A personal writing blog is another effective marketing tool. A blog — short for "weblog" — is basically a journal you post online. You can use it just as you would a journal or writing notebook — except it's available for anyone to read.

Writers may utilize all sorts of blogs ... blogs about their lives, blogs that mix stories and photographs, blogs with essays and other creative writing, blogs that focus on their published pieces of writing. As you consider how to create an effective blog, simply figure out what you want to achieve with it. Then design it appropriately.

A blog also can give you an outlet for your writing, even if you are not getting published elsewhere. Writing every day — or every other day, or once a week — is a good exercise to keep your creative juices flowing.

You can create your own blog free. Or you can spend a little money for a host that offers extra touches, such as advanced layouts, more photo capabilities, and linking tools. Some of the best places to get free blogs include Blogspot.com, Typepad.com, and Livejournal.com. You can find more by simply web-searching for "free blog hosts."

Thousands of blogs operate in the Web-osphere on any number of topics. Some are simply well-written (such as www.thepioneerwoman.com), some are about books and reading (such as www.bookslut.com/.blog), some are on the writing life (such as www.writersdigest.com/editor-ogs/poetic-asides), and some are the blogs of individual writers (such as www.journal.neilgaman.com). You can find thousands of blogs online by Googling the blog topic you're interested in — such as travel blogs, cooking blogs, author blogs, and marketing blogs.

Facebook, Twitter, and Other Social Networking Tools

Social networking has changed the way people do business, develop relationships, keep in contact with other people, stay informed, and live their lives on many levels. It makes it possible for people, using a variety of websites, to share content, develop communities, and interact with one another.

Social networking — especially through the use of Facebook (which has more than 250 million active users) and various online communities — has also changed the way writers do their business. Writers use social networks to come up with ideas, find writing assignments, meet editors, interact with other writers, and promote their work.

If you don't have a presence online already, you need to establish one — primarily because in today's writing culture it's the thing to do. Once you're networked in, you'll wonder how you ever got by before.

Think about the following ways you can utilize Facebook and other communities to market yourself.

- Post links to published articles
- Post news about articles you're working on
- Gain information from fellow community users — whom you can use as sources for your writing, or as extensions of your marketing
- Keep up-to-date with magazine news by "friending" or "liking" magazine pages
- Network with editors
- Promote appearances and other events you may attend that relate to your writing

Vanessa Griggs Davis is one of the best social-networking writers around. She is a freelancer who has jumped into the world of romance writing and has become a successful novelist. Each day on her Facebook page she posts about things in her writing life. She may post about a book signing she's doing, or some news tidbit about the world of writing, or about the progress of her latest project. She has more than 5,000 friends — all who apparently love to read about her writing activities. She's inspiring to writers, and her online activity is evidence of how effective writers can market themselves on the 'Net. You just have to spend the necessary time and energy in doing it.

Another valuable tool is Twitter, a social networking system based at twitter.com. *PC Magazine* defines it as "a very popular instant messaging system that lets a person send brief text messages up to 140 characters in length to a list of followers. Launched in 2006, Twitter was designed as a social network to keep friends and colleagues informed throughout the day. However, it became widely used for commercial and political purposes to keep customers, voters and fans up-to-date as well as to encourage feedback."

Millions of people — celebrities, athletes, businessmen, ordinary people — use Twitter and follow others on Twitter. Freelance writers can use it as an effective marketing tool.

Consider using Twitter as a way to follow magazine editors and others in the publishing field, as well as to post news about your own writing activities.

Multiple Marketing

One of the most common questions that new writers have about article ideas and manuscript submission is this: "May I submit the same article to more than one magazine?" The answer is an emphatic YES — with a few stipulations. By offering your articles to more than one magazine, you can practice one of the most effective marketing methods available to feature writers: *multiple marketing*.

You always must be a professional, ethical writer. Therefore, you should never submit the identical article to more than one competing magazine. Competing magazines are those that have the same audience, such as *Family Circle* and *Woman's Day* or *ESPN the Magazine* and *Sports Illustrated*. You can, however, have the same article published in non-competing magazines, and you can sell reprints of your article to other magazines after the first one has published it.

Most importantly, you can take the same article idea and slant it in slightly (or largely) different ways to different magazines.

Slanting a topic is an important skill to learn if you want to be an expert marketer of your work. By taking a different angle on a topic to make an article fit in with a different audience and magazine, you can get the most out of the work you have done on your article. You can also make more money from your writing.

Freelance writers may sell a piece as many times as possible. To do so, you must learn the following two techniques of multiple marketing:

Learn about all the possible magazines for publication.

This point goes back to one of the foundational concepts we've talked about throughout this book: Be a student of the markets. Always be aware of the various outlets available to you. If you automatically think first of the national magazines, take the opportunity to dig a little deeper. Which local or regional magazines might be interested? Which specialty publications might be appropriate?

Here's a real-life example of how this approach works:

Several years ago, a young woman from Alabama won the Miss America contest. She had all the usual requirements to win a beauty pageant — beauty, poise, and talent — but she also had a unique characteristic. She was deaf. In thinking about her as a potential article topic, a freelance writer imagined how varied the markets could be. The writer proposed the story to women's magazines, teen magazines, beauty magazines, Alabama and Southern magazines, pageant magazines, and disabilities magazines. By slanting the topic to the different aspects of her life, the writer sold the article many times over to different magazines.

Learn as many angles as possible about your topic.

To identify which magazines are good markets, you must know different angles to your topic. If, for example, you were writing an article on "Homegrown Herbs," you'd think about the different people who might have an interest in herbs or gardening: cooks, gardeners, people with environmental interests, homeowners, and women.

To learn these different angles, you must perfect your skills as a researcher and an interviewer. Never approach a topic or person from only one angle. Research intensely to know your topic inside and out, and ask your subject a wide variety of questions, not just the main ones at hand. You will discover the different ways you can slant the articles you want to write.

Give Editors What They Want: "7 Magic Marketing Tips"

It should be obvious by now that marketing is one of the most important techniques to learn in order to achieve publishing success. A talented writer can remain an undiscovered, unpublished one if she does not know how to approach magazine markets or cannot make herself marketable to editors.

To be an expert marketer, learn the following seven "magic" tips:

1. Make sure your idea is marketable.

If your idea doesn't fit any magazines, then it is not a worthwhile idea to pursue. Make your ideas be the types that editors and readers want to read!

2. Be aggressive and confident in finding markets.

Utilize all the tools at your disposal — such as market guides and the Internet — and be aggressive in finding possible markets. If you come up with a good idea and then identify places to submit it, that's great. But you have to take the next step and hit "Send" on the e-query and actively pursue an editor.

3. Get the editor's attention.

Do everything you can to capture an editor's attention. The best way to do that is to propose an idea that the editor just cannot resist. Research the magazine, come up with an article idea that fits it to a tee, and then present the idea to the editor in an effective, professional way. Write a gangbuster query letter, present it to the editor in the proper way, and then be confident in your presentation. Get the editor's attention — and get an assignment.

4. Be creative in spreading the word about your work.

Confidently let people know that you are a magazine writer. Spread the word about yourself and your work. Hand out business cards. Volunteer to do speaking engagements. Query editors and other media types in your community and elsewhere. Use Facebook, Twitter, and other social media to get the word out. Set up a website about your writing. Do whatever you need to do to market your skills.

5. Don't market just once.

Remember that once is never really quite enough. To get the most out of an article idea, market it repeatedly. Think of the various slants to a topic that you can sell to various magazines. Sell an article as a reprint to a second — and third and fourth — magazine. Sell it to the magazine's online site as well. Market, market, and market again!

6. Keep track of your marketing efforts.

An organized writer is a more productive and efficient writer, and this principle is especially true when it comes to your marketing efforts. Develop a plan to keep track of each article you write. Using either a handwritten system or a computer system, record when and where you submit your articles. A spreadsheet program works well for tracking your work. Know where each article is at each stage in the process of getting published. Keep track also of any marketing arrangements or efforts and expenses you make. And be sure to keep track of payments and other successes!

7. Don't let fear get in your way.

President Franklin Roosevelt's quote "The only thing we have to fear is fear itself" is famous for one main reason: *It is true.* As a magazine writer, do not let fear get in the way of your marketing efforts. Believe in your writing, stick to your efforts, realize success will take time and perseverance, and don't let fear of either the unknown or failure get in the way of reaching your goals.

These tips really aren't so much magic. They just require commitment to the process and perseverance to finish it.

Exercises

1. Make a list of 10 magazines for which you are interested in writing or that you particularly like to read.

a.   f.

b.   g.

c.   h.

d.   i.

e.   j.

2. Familiarize yourself with *Writer's Market.* Study the magazines to get a feel for the types of articles they accept from freelancers. Choose one of the magazine entries and analyze all the information that *Writer's Market* provides.

3. Select an article idea that you have already developed while reading this book, or come up with a separate one entirely. Devise five different slants on the same topic.

    a.

    b.

    c.

    d.

    e.

4. Take that same article idea and, using *Writer's Market*, list 10 magazines to which it could be marketed.

a.	f.
b.	g.
c.	h.
d.	i.
e.	j.

5. Locate writers' guidelines online by searching through an online database (at www.writersmarket.com or www.writingfordollars.com). Print out the guidelines for magazines for which you might be particularly interested in writing.

6. Write a list of five goals you have for marketing your work, including specific tasks that you want to accomplish.

    a.

    b.

    c.

    d.

    e.

9

Query Letters

WHAT YOU WILL LEARN IN THIS CHAPTER

• A query letter is the best way to convince an editor that an article idea is right for the magazine.

• Query letters save both the feature writer and the editor time.

• A query letter has four parts: an attention-getting introduction, details of the article, information about the writer, and a closing.

• A query letter must be marketed to the proper publication, mechanically correct, and professional in appearance.

• Queries may be submitted by traditional mail or email.

• Queries can result in nothing, a rejection, a go-ahead, or an assignment.

Talk with a successful freelance writer for more than five minutes, and one term will inevitably come up. It is one of the most important steps you must learn as you start marketing your articles. Mastering it is vital to a freelancer's success in getting published.

Many new writers, though, are intimidated by it. They sincerely want to write for magazines but nevertheless balk at it. They worry that they won't do it correctly, or that an editor will reject them after they've worked so hard at it.

What is it?

It's the *query letter*. In plain language, a query letter is a proposal for an article that a freelancer sends an editor. It is a critical, essential part of the business of freelancing. Even though many wannabe writers see it as a major hurdle, writing good query letters is straightforward and easy to learn.

Aspiring freelancers sometimes are surprised to hear that they must write query letters. "You mean you write a letter and not the entire article?" The process seems backward to them, like going to a ball before putting on a tux. But writing a query letter will save a great deal of time, and it's what the editor wants.

Queries are important for several reasons:

1. They are what most magazines demand.

Yes, a few editors like to get complete manuscripts, but most want query letters. Freelancers should always do what an editor expects. By not following a publication's guidelines, a writer reveals herself to be unprofessional.

2. They save the editor time.

An editor can read a one-page synopsis of an article idea much quicker than a complete article. Working at a job that places demands on time, she is able to make a quicker decision about an article idea.

3. They save the writer time.

By writing a query letter, you are saving yourself a lot of time that you would otherwise spend writing a complete article. A query letter keeps you from wasting time and energy on an article that no magazine might ever accept.

Let's consider the importance of query letters from the perspective of those who know best — real-world editors and experienced writers.

Queries, explains Moira Allen, the owner and administrator of the popular writing website Writing-World.com, are important for a variety of reasons.

"Queries benefit both editors and writers," she says. "Editors much prefer to review a one-page letter than a 10-page manuscript, so queries spend less time in the slush pile. They also enable an editor to determine, quickly, whether you can write effectively, have a coherent, well-thought-out idea that fits the publication's content, have a basic grasp of grammar and spelling, have read the publication, have the credentials or expertise to write the article, and are professional in your approach to writing."

Full-time freelancer Kelly James-Enger, who has written for such magazines as *Cosmopolitan* and *Bride's*, says it's a challenge to make your query letter stand apart from others. To get a letter read and an idea accepted, writers must prepare a well-researched, well-written, efficient query.

"Editors at national magazines receive hundreds of queries every week, but the competition isn't as bad as you might think," she says. "At least 80% of the queries they receive simply aren't targeted to the magazine's readership. Pitch an idea that will interest readers — and show why they will care — and you're halfway there."

The way to make a query letter stand out from others, James-Enger advises, is to offer plenty of "extras" to the editor — such as photographs, sidebars, and source lists. "When I pitch a story, I suggest possible sidebars, quizzes, resource boxes, and other pieces to complement the main piece," she says. "I give [the editor] an idea of whom I plan to interview and suggest a word count."

Make it easy for the editor to accept an idea, James-Enger says. Give her all the important information about your proposed piece so that she can visualize how the article will look and read. "If she likes my idea, and my angle, all she has to do is pick up the phone and assign the piece. Think like your editor, and offer her a package that will make her job easier. You're more likely to get the assignment."

Of course, if you want to take the time to write a complete article for yourself, that is fine. Just be sure to send only a query letter to the editor.

Before You Write a Query Letter

Your goal with a query letter is to convince the editor to accept an article idea. Before writing that winning query, though, you need to do five important tasks. They are the following:

1. Make sure the idea fits the magazine to which you plan to propose the idea.

Chapter 7 discussed this point. If you need, go back and reread the discussion on pages 91-95. The point is so important that it is worth repeating. Spend enough time researching markets for your article idea to assure that you are sending your query letter to an appropriate magazine. Don't waste your time writing the query letter for a magazine that's not a good market.

2. Do enough preliminary research on the topic to allow you to write a thorough and convincing query letter.

You should never write an article before you write a query letter — because you want to know first that an editor is interested in an article before you spend your time writing it. However, you DO need to know a lot about the article. You need to know enough about the topic so that your query letter includes all the basic information needed for the proposed article — the different points you will discuss, the sources you will use, the reasoning for why your article is important, and other details.

That requires you to do adequate preliminary research. At the very least, you probably will have to perform some Internet research, talk to some sources, and outline your proposed article.

3. Write a preliminary outline (or other bare-bones plan) for your article.

Go ahead and start thinking about how the article will be structured. That process will help you understand the article better and will make it easier to write the article once a magazine accepts the idea. You don't have to write a complex outline. You can just make a list of points you plan to cover in the article.

4. Check and double-check the magazine and editor information.

Nothing will get a query letter unread or tossed in the trash can quicker than mistakes such as sending it to the wrong editor, sending it to the wrong address, or misspelling the editor's name. Find out the editor to whom to submit the query letter. Get the information from the magazine's writing guidelines or by contacting the magazine itself. Then address your letter correctly.

5. Make sure you can actually write the article.

There is no worse feeling than the one you get after you receive a go-ahead on your idea and then realize, "Oh my goodness. Now I really have to write this article, and I'm not sure I can or even want to." Before you query, be sure your proposed article is one you really can write and that you will enjoy writing.

Parts of a Query Letter

A query letter — whether it is sent through regular mail or by e-mail — consists of four parts. Each part runs either one or two paragraphs in length, with the letter never exceeding one page in length. The four parts all work together to create a cohesive letter.

1. An Attention-getting Introduction

Don't begin by just coming out and saying, "Would you be interested in an article about castles in Europe?" Instead, introduce the topic in an interesting way

— perhaps by describing one of the castles or by asking some interesting questions about them. The important thing is to capture the editor's interest from the very first line. Make the idea intriguing so that the editor wants to know more about the story you're proposing.

See the *Writing Advantage* feature "The Query Letter Hook" on pages 122-123 for tips on writing an attention-getting introduction.

2. The Basics of the Article

The editor needs to know as much as possible about the proposed article. Tell what the article's theme is. What are the main points you will cover? If you have six or seven points, briefly list them all. Provide a tentative title. Name the sources you plan to use. Give an approximate word count. Tell whether you can include photographs. The editor needs to understand the article you're offering. Don't leave him asking, "Is Cheryl going to include something else about this part of the topic?" or "Why isn't she talking to expert Smith?" Don't leave the editor wondering about anything.

3. A Little about Yourself

This part of the letter offers your chance to tell the editor why you should write this article for her. If you are a freelancer and already have published credits, mention them. If you haven't been published before, though, don't worry about it. Do NOT say, "I have not been published before." Be positive. Give reasons why you're qualified to write the article — such as personal experience with the topic, professional expertise in the area, or access to sources.

4. A Closing

End the query letter by thanking the editor for his time and saying you look forward to hearing back about your proposal. If you are submitting by postal mail, note that you are including an SASE — a self-addressed stamped envelope — for his reply. Make the closing short, courteous, and professional.

After the Query Is Written

After finishing the letter, but before you put it in the mailbox or email it, ask yourself these quick questions:

- Does my query letter provide adequate details about my proposed idea?
- Is my letter interesting to read?

The Query Letter Hook
by Moira Allen

Your first line should grab an editor's attention. It must demonstrate that you can write effectively and that you understand your market.

There are several ways to approach the "hook," including:

The problem/solution hook. This defines a problem or situation common to the publication's audience, then proposes an article that can help solve that problem. Here's an example:

The pet magazine market is an ideal place for newer writers to "break in." However, it is constantly flooded with inappropriate submissions. To break in, one must understand what these magazines want, and what they won't accept. ("Writing for Pet Magazines," sold to *Byline*.)

The informative hook. This usually presents two or three lines of useful information (e.g., facts, statistics), followed by an explanation of how this applies to the target audience. For example:

Thanks to a translation glitch, Microsoft was forced to pull its entire Chinese edition of Windows 95 from the marketplace. Microsoft recovered — but that's the sort of mistake few small businesses can afford! ("How to Localize Your Website," sold to *Entrepreneur's Home Office*.)

The question. Often, this is a problem/solution or informative hook posed as a question, such as:

Did you know ...?

What would you do if ...?

Have you ever wondered ...?

The personal experience/anecdote. Many writers like to take a personal approach, as it immediately establishes the credential of "experience." Be sure, however, that your market uses more personal articles, or first-person accounts, before attempting a hook like this:

Forget-me-nots. I love their wistful name. I love their tiny blue flowers. And yes,

---

• Does my letter match up well with the magazine I am sending it to?

• If I were the magazine's editor, would I want to buy this article?

• Are there any grammar, spelling, or punctuation mistakes?

• Have I eliminated all other mistakes, and is the letter as professional looking and sounding as possible?

See the *Writing Advantage* feature "Query Letter Checklist" on page 124 for

I love that growing them is as simple as pie. ("Forget-me-nots: Simply Unforgettable Spring Flowers," by Mary R., sold to *Fine Gardening*.)

The attention-grabber. The goal of this type of hook is to make the reader sit up and take notice — hopefully long enough to read the rest of the story. This might be a good "hook" for a query about parachuting in Yosemite:

As I fell from the top of Yosemite's El Capitan, I wondered if my life would truly flash before my eyes — or if I would stop screaming long enough to notice.

Hooks to Avoid

Certain hooks scream "amateur" and are guaranteed to speed a query to the rejection pile, including:

The personal introduction. Never start with a line like "Hi, my name is John, and I'd like to send you an article about...." Don't offer irrelevant information, such as "I'm a housewife and mother of three lovely children. Recently I decided to pursue my lifelong dream of writing...."

The "suck-up" hook. Yes, editors want to know that you've read their publication, but they also want you to prove it by offering an appropriate query — *not* by saying, "I've been a subscriber for 20 years and just *love* your magazine...." This hook is even less effective if your query goes on to prove that you've never actually *read* the magazine!

The "bid for sympathy." Don't tell an editor that you've never been published before, or that you need to sell this piece or your children will starve.

The "I'm perfect for you" hook. Never sing your own praises: "I am a highly experienced professional and will be an asset to your magazine." Don't inform the editor that your article is "perfect" for his readers. Never declare that your article is "wonderful" or "fascinating." Prove it — with a good query.

The "I'm an amateur" hook. Never announce that you have never been published before, or that you've tried to sell the same article to 20 other magazines, or that your writing teacher (or mother or spouse) suggested that you send your proposal to a magazine. Even if you haven't sold anything before, you can still *act* like a professional.

(Adapted from "How to Write a Successful Query Letter" by Moira Allen, in www. writing-world.com. Reprinted with permission.)

---

a more detailed list of points.

Now ... send out that query letter!

A Winning E-query

In today's technology-driven world, the e-query has replaced the traditional query letter (mailed through regular mail) for the majority of freelance writers

Query Letter Checklist

Before you submit your query letter to a magazine, assure that you've done the following:

_____ Use the proper format (your name, address, page margins, etc.)

_____ Include your return address

_____ Include information on the specific magazine the query is for (title, address, editor's name, etc.)

_____ Begin with an interesting, thematic first paragraph

_____ Explain clearly what your specific idea is

_____ Slant your idea to the magazine

_____ Don't overuse first person ("I")

_____ Don't be presumptuous, telling the editor what his/her readers will enjoy

_____ Suggest a general word length

_____ Be sure the word length fits the magazine's guidelines

_____ Indicate you are flexible on the word length

_____ Include a statement about your sources for the proposed article

_____ Indicate your qualifications to write the article

_____ Indicate that you are enclosing an SASE (if you query by traditional mail)

_____ Be neat and correct in your typing

_____ Avoid mechanical language errors (spelling, punctuation, sentence structure, etc.)

---

and magazine editors. Find out, of course, if the publication accepts e-queries by reading its writing guidelines. Don't send one if the magazine accepts only "snail mail" queries.

An e-query is identical to a traditional letter in its concept and basic information. Both are written for the same reason, and both include the four parts of a query letter outlined above.

An e-query should have an attention-getting introduction, detailed information about the article, information about yourself, and a closing. Like the mailed letter, it needs to be short, although you can go a little over a "page" with an e-query (since you aren't actually using pages). Be conscientious, though, about the length and keep the query brief. Write your query letter in a Word document, assuring that it stays around one page in length, and then copy it into an email.

Despite their similarities, an e-query differs from a traditional query in the following important features.

1. An e-query is sent as the body of an email.

Don't *attach* the query letter to an email! If you do, an editor might accidentally delete your message, thinking it is spam or junk mail.

2. An e-query has a subject line that identifies it as a query letter.

Identify your message as a query, and then write a short tagline that hints at what your proposed article idea is — something like this: Query Letter: 10 Tips for Budget Back-to-School Shopping.

3. An e-query moves the writer's contact information from the top to the bottom of the query.

In a traditional query letter, business-letter form is followed, and contact information is at the top of the page. The letterhead includes your name, address, phone number, and email address. In an e-query, that information goes at the end of the letter.

4. An e-query sometimes has a signature ("sig") line added to the end of the contact information — although it is optional.

A sig line might say something like "Will Wright, freelance writer with more than 100 articles in print" and might include links to relevant websites, blogs, or other online presence.

5. An e-query may include links to your previously published works.

Editors often like to see, or even request to see, "clips" of your work. Clips are usually photocopied pages of articles you've had published in other magazines or newspapers. They give an editor evidence of your writing proficiency and your publishing experience. With an e-query, you obviously can't include photocopied pages. You can, however, provide links to sites where your work has been published in online versions of magazines. Such links make it easy for an editor to view your work.

Some Warnings about E-queries

While e-queries make it easier and faster to send proposals to editors, you need to keep some important points in mind when you write them.

Make sure the chosen publication accepts e-queries. While 90% or so of magazines prefer e-queries, that leaves 10% that don't. Find out what a specific magazine's policy is. If the editor wants a traditional query letter, send her one. If she wants an e-query, send her one. If she doesn't even want a query letter and prefers to receive a complete manuscript, send her the manuscript. The best way to find out a magazine's policy about e-queries is to read its entry in *Writer's Market* or its writing guidelines.

Just because an e-query can be sent quickly doesn't mean an editor will respond to it immediately. Editors like to take their time reading and considering a proposal. So don't expect to hear back at once. A magazine's writing guidelines will provide information about how long it takes an editor to respond to a query letter. For many magazines, that time is two to six weeks. Don't be surprised if it takes that long to get a response to your e-query.

Write an e-query in as professional a manner as a traditional query letter. Technology, email, social networking, and other forms of quick communication have made it common practice to forego writing etiquette and professionalism. We often write in sentence fragments or use abbreviations instead of complete words. Remember, though, that you must maintain a professional demeanor in your e-queries. Strive for the same perfection you would in a traditional query.

If you use e-queries properly, they offer many benefits and can increase your chances of publication.

Results of Your Query Letter

A query letter — either a traditional letter or an e-query — can result in several different scenarios. It will get you one of the following responses:

1. Nothing

Sometimes when you submit a query letter, you will wait — and wait, and wait some more — for a response from an editor. And you will never hear anything. Most freelance writers, including successful ones, sometimes get no response to their queries. It can be frustrating, but recognize it as part of the business of freelancing. The reason for no response can be as simple as the fact that the mail isn't running properly, or the magazine has a huge backlog of queries, or an editor has lost your query. You can deal with no response in either of two ways: Either chalk it up to a missed opportunity, or after about six weeks send a brief follow-up letter or email to inquire about the status of your idea.

2. Rejection

There is always a chance that an editor will reject your proposed article. You may receive a personalized letter that spells out why your idea was not accepted, or you might receive a form letter with a box simply checked with the reason for the rejection, or even a small piece of photocopied paper saying something such as "Your idea does not meet our present needs. We send form rejections because we don't have time to reply personally to each query."

Some rejections are more polite than others, but they still sting. They make you question what you're doing and if you're doing it correctly.

The important thing to remember with rejections, though, is that there is a reason why you received one. Figure out why you got a rejection. Was it that your query letter had a problem, your idea didn't fit the market, the magazine had covered your idea recently, or some other reason? Then try to learn from the rejection. If you have a good idea, propose it to another magazine; or come up with another idea and send it to a different magazine.

3. Go-ahead

When an editor wants to see a proposed article, she will give a "go-ahead." In essence, she will say, "Yes, this is a good idea for an article. Go ahead and send us the article for consideration." After you receive a go-ahead, write your article and submit it to the same editor. She will then have another decision to make: whether to accept your article and publish it. Remember that a go-ahead isn't a promise that the magazine will publish the article. It simply indicates that the editor is interested. However, if you get a go-ahead, the chances are good that the editor will accept your article if it delivers on what you promised in your query.

4. Firm Assignment

When editors are interested in a proposed article, most issue a go-ahead — which means the writer will still have to wait for a final round of either rejection or acceptance. On occasion, though, an editor will issue a firm assignment, instead of a go-ahead, to a writer who has a track record that shows she can produce a publishable article. A firm assignment indicates that a writer has come up with an idea that is particularly timely for the magazine or has hit upon a particular interest for the editor. In such a case, the editor will request the proposed article for a specific issue of the magazine. The writer signs a contract and is guaranteed a publication. It is unlikely that a new writer would ever get a contract in advance of writing an article, but it is possible for beginning writers to build up a resumé of published articles and to get assignments soon.

Query Letter Examples

To help you learn to write a successful query letter, on pages 129-132 are letters to provide some examples. All of them are successful examples, because each resulted in a go-ahead from a magazine editor and in a published article.

The examples include two traditional query letters (letters popped into the mailbox and sent to an editor) and two e-queries. Note that the writing style and letter construction are similar in both types. The traditional letters could easily be made into e-queries, and vice versa.

Exercises

1. Read each of the four query letter examples on the following pages of this chapter and provide a point-by-point outline of each one.

2. Of the four sample query letters, which letter do you think is the best one? Why?

3. Select an article idea you developed from Chapter 7 and write a traditional query letter about it.

4. Take the same idea you selected in Exercise 3 and write an e-query for it.

Traditional Query Letter #1

June 11, 2013

Hope Daniels, Editor
Military Lifestyle
1730 Wisconsin Ave. NW
Washington, DC 20007

Dear Ms. Daniels,

With each new school year, parents have to work with their children's teachers with problems such as a child's hyperactivity, illness, or poor grades.

Good parent-teacher communication plays an important role in our educational process. For military parents who move frequently, it is sometimes difficult to establish and maintain good parent-teacher relationships. Often parents don't know how and when to contact their children's teachers. Once they get in touch with teachers, they often do not know how to communicate effectively with them.

I have in mind an article of approximately 1,500 words on how military parents can have a good parent-teacher relationship. "How To Have a Healthy Parent-Teacher Relationship" would cover the following points: (1) Take an interest in your child's education, (2) Meet the teacher early in the year, (3) Attend parent-teacher conferences, (4) Maintain contact throughout the year, and (5) Have realistic expectations.

Anecdotes, examples and quotes based on my experience as a former high school teacher and as a parent of two children would be included. I would also include quotes from military parents on their experiences with their children's teachers.

I also can provide two sidebars: (1) suggestions for a successful parent-teacher conference and (2) books about the parent-teacher relationship.

A freelance writer and book author, I have had articles published in *Living with Teenagers*, *Gifted Children Monthly*, *Focus on the Family*, *The Lion Magazine*, *The Optimist Magazine*, *The Rotarian*, *Good Reading*, *Mature Years*, *Hoosier Schoolmaster*, *Directions*, and other magazines.

I'm enclosing an SASE for your reply. Thank you so much for considering my idea for your magazine. I look forward to hearing from you.

Sincerely,
[Signature]
Ima W. Riter
P. O. Box 123
Anywhere, TX 75477
e-mail: imawriter@quomari.com

Traditional Query Letter #2

June 11, 2013

Ms. Jane Fort
Articles Editor
Teen Magazine
3000 Ocean Park Blvd.
Santa Monica, CA 90405

Dear Ms. Fort,

In many high schools, the weekend football game is just as important to the coeds as to the players on the team. Yelling and screaming have become as American as the high school band. They can also be dangerous to one's health.

The cartwheel spinning cheerleader, the cardholder in the cheering section, and the otherwise demure sophomore urging on her favorite player need not warm the bench at the Victory Dance or sound like Tugboat Annie the next week at school.

I have in mind an article of about 1,500 words on how to cheer and yell safely, based on the advice of two leading authorities on the subject.

Cheer. Yell.... But don't scream. That's the advice of Dr. Leonard Spicer, professor of speech at Hoopla University. Each year he coaches newly elected cheerleaders in the art of yelling without damaging the vocal bands. Dr. Phillip Roosevelt, speech correctionist from Atlanta, Ga., works with the same problem and is available for an interview for the story.

Should you be interested in the idea, I would be happy to emphasize any particular points you might especially like to see in the article.

I work for the campus newspaper at Hoopla University and have written a number of feature articles dealing with physical therapy and with campus life.

Thank you for considering my idea. For your convenience, I've included an SASE for your reply.

Sincerely,
[Signature]
Ima W. Riter
P. O. Box 123
Anywhere, TX 75477
e-mail: imawriter@quomari.com

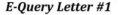
E-Query Letter #1

[In email subject line] Query Letter: Everything's Coming Up Cupcakes

Dear Ms. Jones:

Cupcakes, it seems, are everywhere these days. You see them on t-shirts, and on book covers, and in the hands (and mouths) of celebrities. They are quite chic and trendy!

Cupcakes, however, are not just trendy. They are a classic treat that have been a part of children's birthday parties for years. And for good reason ... they're cost-efficient, portable, relatively easy to make, and fun to eat.

I have in mind an article for *Treasure Valley Family* tentatively titled "Everything's Coming Up Cupcakes," which would give practical and fun ideas for using cupcakes in your child's next birthday celebration. The article would be tailored for your upcoming November issue on birthday and holiday celebrations.

The article would include my Top Ten Celebration Cupcakes, which are all based on using cake mixes and yet are creative and fun. This list would include such creations as my Tie-Dye Cupcakes, Cookies 'n Cream Cupcakes, Popcorn Cupcakes, Flower Cupcakes, and Zoo Cupcakes. Quick and easy directions for each of the cupcakes would be provided, and photographs could be provided as well. The article would also include recipes for my three "go to" homemade frostings — Buttercream Frosting, Chocolate Buttercream Frosting, and Cream Cheese Frosting. I could also provide a sidebar on quick and easy ways to display birthday party cupcakes in a fun way — such as making a cupcake tower, making a "cake" out of cupcakes, etc.

If interested in my article, I can have it ready for you as soon as you need it.

I am a freelance writer who has had articles published in such parenting publications as *Atlanta Parent, Living with Teenagers, Family Fun, West Virginia Family, ParentLife,* and *Memphis Parent.* As the mother of three daughters, I have made countless cupcakes for many birthday parties over the years. I often blog about my baking creations, which you can read at www.imawriter.blogspot.com.

Thank you for considering my article for *Treasure Valley Family*. I'll look forward to hearing from you soon.

Sincerely,
Ima W. Riter
P. O. Box 123
Anywhere, TX 75477
e-mail: imawriter@quomari.com

Ima W. Riter
"A freelancer for all your writing needs"
Visit me at www.imawriter.blogspot.com and on Facebook and Twitter

E-Query Letter #2

[In email subject line] Query Letter: Hometown Spotlight on Helen Keller Home

Dear Ms. Sewell:

In a world full of chirping birds and laughing children, she heard nothing. In a world full of beautiful vistas and unique scenes, she saw nothing. And in this world, she was unable to communicate. Still, this amazing woman conquered all odds to become one of the most famous, successful, and inspiring Americans to ever live. Today, visitors can become inspired all over again by touring her childhood home and reliving the miracles that happened there.

That woman is, of course, Helen Keller, and her childhood home can be found in inconspicuous Tuscumbia, Alabama.

Would you be interested in an article tentatively titled "Where Miracles Happen" for your "Hometown Spotlight" department? The article would include such information as compelling stories about Helen Keller, descriptions of the home and the accompanying guest house (where Keller's teacher, Anne Sullivan, had her first breakthrough with young Helen), stories about the famous water pump on the property, descriptions of the museum housed there, and tourist information about visiting the home. I plan on interviewing the home's curator and Keller's great niece (who is a city leader in Tuscumbia). The article would run approximately 800 words in length, although I can vary it according to your needs. I also plan on taking photographs.

I am a freelance writer with more than 1,000 published articles to my credit. You may click on the following links to read travel articles I've written for various newspapers and magazines: www.atlantaparent.com/gulfshores, www.matureliving.com/callawayg, and www.countryroad.com/imawriter. I live in Birmingham, Alabama, which is just a short drive to Tuscumbia.

Thank you for considering my article idea for *American Profile*. I look forward to hearing from you.

Sincerely,
Ima W. Riter
P. O. Box 123
Birmingham, AL 34567
e-mail: imawriter@quomari.com

Ima W. Riter
"A freelancer for all your writing needs"
Visit me at www.imawriter.blogspot.com and on Facebook and Twitter

10

Research and Interviews

WHAT YOU WILL LEARN IN THIS CHAPTER

• Research is the heart of the feature article. It should include written and human sources.

• The three main types of research are primary research, secondary research, and personal experiences/insight.

• Research comes in both traditional printed form and computerized form. It often includes library research and online searches.

• Interviews are a vital part of research. They involve three steps: preparing for the interview, conducting the interview, and following up after the interview.

• The best quotes gained from interviews are original, poignant, and integral to the article's theme.

*A*t the heart of feature writing is research.

Certainly, feature writers can write about what they know, using their own experiences and insight and expertise. But research can't stop there. And with most articles, it can't really begin there either.

Good, effective feature articles rely on quality, sourced material to provide accurate and interesting information. Good information provides the foundation for an article's accuracy and usefulness to the reader. It comes from research.

An article on cutting-edge breast cancer research, for example, is strengthened by information from medical journals, quotes from doctors and researchers, and interviews with breast cancer survivors.

An article on traveling to San Francisco is enhanced by the writer's own insights into the sights and sounds of the city — but interviews with local merchants, residents, and city leaders will give it vitality. Library and computerized research on such details as the city's history and culture will give it fullness.

As you begin work on a feature article, you must consider where to get the best information possible — meaning you will have to do some real legwork. You will need to go to the library and look up the topic in old magazines, go online and search extensively for the best tidbits, talk to experts, and meet with real-life people who have experienced the topic first-hand. In other words, don't scrimp on the research stage — even though it may be tempting to do so.

Types of Research

Before going to sources for information, you must consider the types of research that will work best for your article. The four main categories of research are the following:

Primary Research

The ideal research is primary research. It comes directly from the "horse's mouth" — from a person with first-hand experience ... someone who knows the topic intimately, not someone who has just been told about the topic or who has quoted someone else who knows about the topic. Primary material includes such things as the diary or journal of a person involved in a historical event, an interview with an eyewitness to a crime, and a conversation with the author of a book on your article's topic. Primary research adds accuracy and credibility to feature articles. When you use primary research, readers can be confident that you are providing the best possible information, and they will trust your writing.

Secondary Research

Secondary research relies on someone or something that doesn't have first-hand knowledge of an event or topic. Although it is not as good as primary research, it still can provide quality material. Secondary research includes such things as magazine articles, quotes from a biography, encyclopedia entries, and interviews with someone who knows about an event second-hand (who wasn't actually at the event but heard about it from someone else). While secondary research isn't as immediate as primary research, it still can can have a place in a feature article. Feature writers often use secondary research. When you use it, just make sure your source is a good one, and use secondary material as a complement to primary research.

Interviews

A main component of research for feature writing is interviews. Articles need to include quotes from real people — both experts on your topic and ordinary people who have experience with it. Some quotes will come from a brief phone call to a source to ask a question or two about the topic. Other quotes will come from extensive sit-down interviews with the subject of your article or someone who is deeply involved in the topic.

Interviews are important because readers like to read about other people, and they instinctively trust information that has direct quotes from good sources. If you quote from an expert or someone who otherwise knows about your topic, that information adds interest and validity to your story. The reader feels confident that your information is reliable because of these quotes.

Personal Insight/Experience

While interviews and primary and secondary research are vital to an article, writers often must rely on their own insights and experiences. This is especially true for personal-experience articles and essays.

You can also use your own insight if you're writing a how-to or informational piece on a topic you know well — even though you should incorporate expert sources as well. For example, you could use your experiences in a story about survival after being lost in the mountains. You could use your own insights in a how-to article on weight-loss strategies after losing 100 pounds yourself. Readers like to get information from people with whom they have something in common. Your experiences can allow readers to identify with you.

The type of research you do will depend on the type of article you're writing.

If, for example, you are doing a how-to piece, you will need to research written sources on your topic and talk to experts. From those experts you will get quotes and information. The same thing goes for descriptive pieces, historical articles, personality profiles, and other genres.

If you're writing a personal-experience article or essay, you'll rely mostly on your own knowledge as you write about what happened to you. Still, you may find yourself talking to others who were involved with you, or you might do background research on places or topics that relate to your experience.

Whatever the topic of your article, the key is to have a good balance of research. You need a blend of written sources and expert quotes. You want both hard information — such as facts and figures — and anecdotal material.

Amount of Research

Any article you write will require a considerable amount of research. You need enough information to make your article credible. So on your schedule for doing the article, designate time for research.

Don't overload your article, though, with too many sources. Feature articles are intended to be enjoyable to read and usually have a human-interest angle. Too few sources can damage the information's accuracy, but too many sources can load down an article and make it read like a research paper.

No hard-and-fast rules exist about how many sources to use for a feature article. As a general guideline, though, writers should include a variety of types of sources and probably use at least five. A good principle is to have at least two written sources — either from a website, book, or other material — and at least three live sources, people with whom you have talked. Make sure at least one of the live sources is not a so-called expert but just a "regular" person with experience on your topic. By having at least one real-life, regular source, you will make your article feel more human to readers. Of course, the number of sources can vary according to the article. Just make sure the balance works for your topic.

As you decide on the types of material you need, first think through your article in as much detail as possible. Imagine that you are a reader, and ask yourself what main questions you want answered. What questions would intrigue you? Make a list of all the questions, and then decide what types of information can answer them. Do you need statistics? Quotes from experts? Quotes from "real life" sources? Interesting anecdotes?

Then make another list, this one detailing the different sources of information you plan to track down.

Use the *Writing Advantage* feature "Sources Form" on page 137 for a systematic way to keep track of your research.

Where can you locate the material you need for your article? In answer to that question, let's consider the following sources: the Internet, traditional sources, and people.

The Internet

Search engines, news sites, magazine sites, online documents, government sites,

Sources Form

Keep track of research resources by listing documentary sources (books, articles, websites, etc.) and people interviewed.

Written Source 1:
(e.g., title, author, publisher, page number, or website address)

Written Source 2:

Written Source 3:

Additional Written Sources:

Individual Source 1:
(name, contact information)

Individual Source 2:

Individual Source 3:

Additional Individual Sources:

---

organizational sites, social network sites ... the options are truly immense as you consider the research that can be done online.

The Internet has opened up a treasure chest of opportunities for writers as they do research for feature articles. There are millions of websites filled with unimaginable pieces of material. The research options are nearly limitless — so much so that they seem overwhelming.

At one time, feature writers spent many hours in the library doing research. Now, many find that they can almost exclusively work online. The Internet can provide resources for just about every step of the research process. It is especially good for finding background, general information on most topics. When beginning your research, do an online search using an engine such as Google to find general information on your topic. The Internet is also valuable for locating expert sources. Good places to find experts are university, hospital, and organizational websites.

Following, in more detail, is a list of some of the ways feature writers commonly use the Internet to do research. You will find these approaches easy to use and helpful as you put together the body of material you need for your articles.

1. Use search engines to find initial information.

As you begin research, do a quick and cursory search for information. Use Google, Bing, or any search engine that you prefer. Realize that an Internet search can result in millions of results, so be as specific as possible in your search so that you get the best information related to what you're looking for. If you're writing an article on turtle care for a pet magazine, for example, don't just search for "turtles." Search with more specific phrases, such as "pet turtle aquariums" or "pet turtle hazards" or "pet turtle temperament."

2. Surf to see what else has been written on your topic.

Look at other articles that have been written on your topic, both to get a cursory reading on your topic and to see how you can write something unique.

3. Locate expert sources.

One of the most valuable things about the Internet is its ability to help you find experts whom you otherwise would have to spend massive amounts of time locating. Before the Internet, writers had to search extensively for a doctor, counselor, book author, or other expert to use as a source. Now, you can find experts with a keystroke. You can find sources at personal websites, online university staff listings, organizations' websites, and many other professional sites.

4. Locate real-world sources.

Use the Web to find real-life individuals to quote in stories. You can find these people through message boards and websites that cater to individual interests and then contact them by email.

5. Locate additional resources to use in sidebars.

The most common type of sidebar in magazine articles is a list of resources and recommended readings. Such lists offer readers a place to find more information on the topic. You can use the Web to put together these lists quickly and easily. Make sure the information on each site is current.

We should add that, besides its value for source research, the Internet is invaluable for other reasons as well. Many freelancers use it almost daily to locate magazines, newspapers, online publications, and other places to market their writing. They also use it to communicate with sources, readers, fellow writers, and editors. Countless online resources can help you keep in touch with all of the people who are vital to your success as a freelance writer. You can use writing networks to correspond with fellow writers, get feedback from readers via Facebook, and keep in touch with editors via email and magazine websites.

Traditional Research

Even in the age of the Internet, there still are times when you will find yourself at the local library doing traditional research. A library is especially good for its reference section. There you will find encyclopedias and other reference books to guide you to general information about a topic. Many libraries also have a collection of magazines, where you can often find helpful articles that others have written on your topic. They will give you ideas about your subject and leads to sources you might use in your own articles.

The following sources of research at the library can be especially fruitful:

Reader's Guide to Periodical Literature

This guide, which is organized by years, lists article topics and specific issues of magazines that contain articles on those topics. It is the best place to locate other pertinent consumer magazine articles on your topic. Other guides — such as *Education Index*, *Business Periodicals Index*, and *Religion Index* — list articles in trade and specialized magazines. Many libraries subscribe to services that have converted these guides — which in print form can extend over several shelves — into computerized databases. So they're even easier to use.

Encyclopedias

A wide variety of general encyclopedias, such as *World Book* and *Encyclopedia Brittanica* — as well as specialized encyclopedias geared to specific areas, such as medicine and historical biographies — provide basic information on thousands of topics. The volumes are excellent resources to use as a starting point in your research. They will give you a good overview of a topic and help you in deciding where to go next in your research.

Books

Books will provide more in-depth information about your topic, and often you will find it valuable to sit down with one to get a good overview of your topic. Doing preliminary research in books is especially valuable if an editor has assigned you a topic that you know little about. Just skimming through books can be useful. For example, if you're doing a historical piece, books still provide the best information on historical people and events.

Most libraries have their card catalog system computerized. With access to the Internet, you can search the card catalogue from your home computer. It is easy to locate a book by topic, author, or title. If your local library doesn't have a book in stock, it can usually get the book for you through its Interlibrary Loan System.

Government Sources

Government offices and agencies maintain efficient and cumulative collections of information in many areas. They keep track of an enormous amount of material such as statistics, trends, and all types of findings on topics as wide-ranging as education and health — in fact, on almost any topic you can think of. The reference librarian can help you locate government journals, indexes, and catalogs. Many government bodies have computerized their collections and made them available online.

Other Reference Materials

Hundreds of other encyclopedias, indexes, bibliographies, journals, and other reference guides are available at your local library. College or university libraries usually have a large reference room and can be especially valuable. Take a Saturday to visit the library's reference room. Ask for a tour and ask questions of the reference librarian.

Using People for Research

The best research source for feature articles is people. They should be at the heart of feature writing. By talking to people, and using their information and quotes, you will add a sense of reality to your articles. Readers will connect with your human sources, whether they are experts or ordinary individuals.

Locating human sources is thus of utmost importance.

How does the writer go about finding them? Here are some ways I have located sources for my own writing:

The Internet plays a valuable role. I live near a respected medical center and university, and I rely regularly on their websites to find sources. Whenever I need an expert on a topic, I log onto the university's or the medical center's website and go to its media relations office. The media relations staff has always put me directly in contact with expert sources who were perfect for what I needed. Those sources have provided material for articles about topics as wide ranging as infant brain development, dealing with grief, and summertime eye care.

I also live near several liberal arts colleges, which have provided information on more esoteric topics. For an article on the best holiday movies, I was able to locate a professor at one of the schools who specializes in film history. I simply logged onto the college's website and found a page that listed specializations for various professors and their email addresses.

Universities are great resources, but you also can find sources through organizational, foundation, and business websites.

Furthermore, you can use the Internet to locate ordinary people who have special insight into your topic. For an article on reading to children for a parenting magazine, for example, some literacy experts and educators had already given me material. I wanted to include some stories, though, from real-life moms who valued reading to their children. I logged onto an online community called Momwriters (a group designed for writers who are also mothers) and posted a message about my article. Several members emailed me good quotes, which I included in the published article.

Similarly, Facebook and other social media outlets can be used to locate real-life sources. They are convenient resources for getting usable quotes.

While the Internet can be useful in finding sources, there are still some good "old fashioned" resources that work well. Consider using the following ones.

Books

You can quote authors of books on your topic. Better yet, you can contact the author of a book and interview him for targeted answers to questions you have.

Magazine Articles

The same thing goes for articles about your topic. If the author is an expert, she might be a good person to interview. Most magazines include a bio of the writer at the end of an article. The bio might even include the writer's email address or contact information (and, if it doesn't, you can contact the magazine for the writer's information).

The Yellow Pages

Every town probably has at least one expert on some topic, and most people love to be interviewed for articles. To locate experts, simply use the phone book's Yellow Pages. It's easy to locate psychologists, coaches, painters — any specialists — by looking up their category in the phone book.

People You Know

When searching for sources, don't forget your own circle of friends and family. Simply think about the experiences and expertise these people have. Do you have a teacher aunt who can give special insight about parents working with teachers? Is one of your best friends a lawyer who can provide you with good information on making a will? Is one of your co-workers a marathon runner who can be a source for your article on exercising to stay fit? Family and friends are usually good sources because they are easy to contact and talk to. Also, since most people have friends and family all over the country, using them as sources adds geographical variety to a story.

The Interview Process

Getting information from people means that you must conduct interviews. By talking with people, you can assure that you get the kind of information you need. Select sources who can give you special insight into your topic — ones who will make your articles more credible, trustworthy, and interesting.

Interviews will vary in style and scope. With some stories, you will need only a sentence or two from a source to use within a section of your article. For example, assume you are doing an article on equipment that the novice hiker needs. You could get quotes from an expert hiker, an outdoor store manager, and a park ranger. You wouldn't need to spend extensive time with the sources, but you do need to talk with them long enough to get some good quotes. In such situations, you can stop by a source's office to get a few quotes, or you can phone or email him. The contact method you use will depend on which one he is most comfortable with.

With other articles, though, you may need to do lengthy interviews. Let's say you're doing an article on a local bed and breakfast. You'd want to sit down and talk to the B&B's owners. Or you're working on an article on how churches are becoming more modern and tech-savvy. You'd want to interview a local pastor in person at his church. Or you're doing an article on an up-and-coming country singer touring in your area. You'd want to do a full-length interview with her in person.

For many writers, interviewing is their favorite part of the writing and publishing process. Sources are usually forthcoming and excited to be quoted in an article. So don't worry about talking with people, even famous people. Interviewing them is usually a pleasant experience.

You do need to know certain things, though, about the interviewing process. They will help your interview be enjoyable and, more importantly, productive — so that you get just the type of information you need for your story.

Before the Interview

In preparing to interview someone, keep the following points in mind:

Arrange the interview.

Contact the source to arrange an interview. Be upfront about what you're doing. Tell the person about the article, where it will be published, and other specifics. Then let the source be in control as much as possible about the actual logistics of the interview. Let her pick a place and time that are convenient for her. As for a location, her place of business or home usually works best. Before the interview, be sure to call and remind her of the interview time.

Do background research and prepare questions.

Never go into an interview unprepared. Do enough background research on your topic and learn enough about your interviewee so that you will be well prepared and knowledgeable. Come up with a list of questions to cover all points you want addressed in the interview. Make sure the questions are good, open-ended ones that will spark discussion.

See the *Writing Advantage* feature "Common Types of Interview Questons" on page 144 for some of the most common types of interview questions.

Gather your materials.

Take pens that work (and extra ones as well), a notebook, and a reliable tape recorder (with extra batteries) if you will be recording the interview.

During the Interview

As you do the interview, keep the following points in mind.

Be comfortable and interested.

When you are comfortable with your interviewee, you will get the best re-

Writing Advantage

Common Types of Interview Questions

Break-the-Ice Questions
These questions make you and your interviewee comfortable with each other and can include topics such as the weather, current events, the interviewee's family, an object in the interviewee's office, hobbies, anything you have in common.

Yes-or-No Questions
These questions allow the interviewee simply to answer in one of two ways. There is no elaboration, which usually limits the usefulness of the answer.

Probing Questions
These questions allow you to get more information about a response you received. ("Tell me more about that..." or "Why do you say that is so?")

Hazy Questions
These questions leave the interviewee with too many options not to answer the question. You might ask, for example, about how the person "feels" about a broad topic. Such a question is not specific enough.

Closed Questions
These questions seek specific answers and should deal with points central to your article idea. Instead of the hazy question above, you'd ask something narrower, such as, "How do you think your community will benefit from its new park system?"

---

sponses and will have a good interview experience. Establish rapport with the interviewee at the beginning by talking about something friendly and general. During the body of the interview, sound interested in the person and the topic, pay attention to what the person is saying (rather than, for example, looking at your questions), talk informally, and be willing to go off-subject as unforeseen subjects come up.

Take notes.
Even if you're recording the interview, take notes also. If you're not recording it, then take notes that are comprehensive enough that you will understand them well. Also, develop some sort of shorthand or abbreviation system so that

you are not constantly writing throughout the interview. Make sure you can decipher your own notes. Don't let taking notes distract you. Pay close attention to the interviewee.

Let the interviewee talk.

One of the worst things you can do in an interview is to remain rigid as if you are going by a script. Although you have questions you want answered, don't let them dictate the interview. Notice what the interviewee wants to talk about. In many cases, the best answers you will get are the ones that come when you go off-script. Remember that an interview is not a formal press conference. Think of it as a conversation with a person. Such an approach can lead to important details and interesting stories. Or let the conversation veer off in a different direction than the one you had planned. That approach might lead to quotes that you would have never received otherwise.

Be observant.

Be observant of the environment around you. Notice the things in the setting. Some items may reveal important details about the interviewee. Pictures on an office wall, for example, could indicate something about a person's background or interests. Ask the interviewee about items in his office. Pay attention to the person's mannerisms and dress. Is he well groomed? Is he always moving his hands or gesturing? Or is he completely still and formal? You may have occasion in your article to mention mannerisms or dress if they illustrate a point you are making.

Take a camera.

Take a digital camera with you to interviews. You never know when you might need to take a picture of something you'd like to remember later. Before taking your first picture, though, ask the interviewee for permission.

After the Interview

Once you have completed the interview and are looking for good information and quotes for your article, keep the following points in mind.

Digest the information.

Create a system for digesting and organizing your information. Some people rewrite or transcribe their notes immediately after an interview. Others let the

Terry Wilhite
"Conducting Interviews"

Q: How do you come up with your interview questions?

WILHITE: Let me first say that I think I am always the least effective when I try to be "Mr. Professional Interviewer," and it's difficult not to slip into that role. Sometimes you really can try too hard and over think — or over ask — the interview. The best questions are the ones my senior adult mama would ask or the questions that would come from my 14-year-old son — plain, interesting questions. Quite frankly, sometimes the questions can be so simple they make me feel a little uncomfortable. Again it's the compulsion to be Mr. Professional Interviewer who has a drive to ask "super-intelligent" questions.

The best questions are plain and simple — common sense. It is for this reason that I don't stress when it comes to interview prep. I do want to be comfortable enough that I know basic information about the person and the subject that I'll be covering, but in the interview, I am not the subject expert. The interviewee is. I'm representing Joe Six Pack and asking the questions he'd ask if given the chance.

Q: What is your interview approach?

WILHITE: I hope my interviewees would say it is relaxing. I certainly try to make it that way, and the way I believe that is best achieved is by just being myself, establishing with the interviewee that I'm not especially well-versed on the subject and explaining that they'll have to help me and the listener understand the complicated concepts. That usually helps them feel better because they know now I'm not going to be intimidating.

I usually don't provide the questions to the interviewee prior to recording. Some interviewers do. It's a personal preference. There is never enough time to pack in all the ground we need to cover. So I do try to establish the parameters of the interview beforehand and

---

notes sit for a few hours before doing the transcription. Also look over your notes and make any notations that stand out. For example, circle the really good quotes.

Contact the interviewee if you need to.

Sometimes you may find that you need to follow-up on information after an interview. You might realize that you need more information or that you aren't sure about a fact you wrote down. To prepare for that possibility, at the end of an interview ask the interviewee, "Would you mind if I contact you later if I find I

ask my interviewee to work hard to try to put answers in simple terms.

The best stories contain heart and passion — a great deal of emotion — and to get that result the poignant questions have to be asked. Still, those are simple. I would not start on the emotional deep end of questioning but swim my way there.

Q: What makes a "good" interview or a "bad" interview?

WILHITE: The best interviews are the ones where the interviewee forgets about the recording equipment — television lights, small digital recorder or simple notepad — and he forgets even about a formal interview being conducted. The best interview begins when we've established common ground, rapport, as people.

The worst interviews are those where the interviewee refuses to relax or has an overwhelming compulsion to be an authority and can't abandon the confusing trade speak. Again, the less I try to be Mr. Professional Interviewer, the better chances are for a more down-to-earth response to my questions.

Q: What are some of your favorite tips for doing an effective interview?

WILHITE: My communications mantra is this: When there is common ground, relationships can be established that lead to understanding. The best advice I can give is, as an interviewer, go for the common ground. The common ground for both the interviewee and interviewer is helping the listener/reader understand. Be sensible and methodical and ask the questions your mama would want answered. Most importantly, relax and have fun.

Terry Wilhite is the communications director for a large public school system and is interviewed several hundred times a year for local and national news (appearing on Fox News and *60 Minutes*, among others). He worked for 19 years in corporate communications, where he interviewed people regularly for a monthly industry magazine. He also freelance writes for magazines and produces video blogs of profile interviews.

---

need anything else?" Such a question is a safety valve in the event you do need to recontact the person — so that the interviewee won't think you simply did an inadequate job in the original interview. It is also a wise practice to follow-up with a "thank you" to the source for doing the interview and let her know of publication plans for your article. Such courtesy is not only simple politeness, but it also will serve you well should you ever wish to interview the source for another article.

Think about how to use the information.

Once you've read through and digested your information, think about how it will fit in your article. If you are writing an entire article on the interview subject, you can start writing the article at this point. If the interview will be just one source in a broader article, go ahead and outline the article and decide where you will use the information.

Some Issues with Quotes — and Their Solutions

Feature writers find that sources often make one of three comments to them. They either say, "I'm not sure I really want you to use that quote" (or "This is off the record, right?"), or make the request, "Please clean up what I say to you. I'm not a writer. So make me sound better," or ask, "May I read the article before you print it?"

Each statement is important and poses a challenge for writers. Here are ways to handle them:

If someone asks you not to use a quote, try not to agree right off the bat.

Talk with the person and try to compromise on a quote. Say something such as, "Is there some other way you could phrase it?" or "Is there something related to that point that you would feel comfortable talking about?" The request not to use a quote most commonly comes into play when a person is talking about a controversial issue or about a personal experience that includes other people whom the source does not want to involve. By being open, honest, and willing to work with the source, you should be able to strike a balance. Realize that requests about sensitive quotes are usually easier to handle when writing feature stories for magazines than hard news for newspapers. Newspaper reporters often deal with sensitive or controversial news, which is more likely to cause problems.

If someone wants you to "make me sound better," reassure him that you will.

The main change is usually cleaning up simple grammatical mistakes. The source may say something incorrectly, but correcting it doesn't really change the nature of the information. In that case, it is okay to polish a quote. In some instances, you will want to retain a source's dialect or colorful language. In that situation, you may wish to leave the quote as it is.

If someone asks to read the article before it comes out in print, you should usually say "No."

Getting approval from sources is a taboo for most newspaper reporters, and that is usually the case for feature writers as well. The main reason is that having a source read a manuscript can add greatly to the amount of time required to get it into finished shape. Some people who make such a request do so because they want to control the situation. The request, of course, can create problems for the writer and editor. If, though, the person wants to see the article simply for an innocent reason — for example, because she's never been interviewed before — you may consider compromising and read a quote or a paragraph to her. Gauge each situation on an individual basis, considering both practical and ethical concerns.

The Best Quotes

The end result of interviews will be a collection of quotes that may or may not be usable in your article. Some quotes will be high quality and fit your article perfectly. Others will not be distinctive or informative enough to use. You don't have to use everything that you get from a source.

Quotes in an article should be interesting, revealing, and important to the article as a whole.

The best quotes have the following characteristics:

1. They are original.

The best quotes reveal information that could not be acquired easily from another source. Some statements that an interviewee makes might be so general that you could get them from almost anywhere. Don't quote the interviewee for such information. Paraphrase it. You shouldn't, for example, quote the interviewee for a statement such as "Washington, D.C., is the capital of the United States." Make sure you use quotation marks only for statements that are original.

2. They have emotional power.

The best quotes don't need to make the reader cry or laugh hysterically, but they do pack a punch. They are powerful, or humorous, or revealing, or poignant, or filled with information.

3. They are integral to the article's theme.

The best quotes are ones that directly relate to the article's theme or topic. If a quote does not fit clearly with the main idea of the article, don't use it.

Exercises

1. Take a trip to your local library and orient yourself to its resources. List five sources you foresee using in your feature writing.

    a.

    b.

    c.

    d.

    e.

2.. Select an article idea for which you have already written a query letter (and one that you want to write an article about), and make a list of research sources you will use for it. Include two written sources, two expert human sources, and two real-life "ordinary" people.

    a. Written source:

    b. Written source:

    c. Expert source:

    d. Expert source:

    e. Ordinary person:

    f. Ordinary person:

3. Contact an individual to interview. The person may be someone you know — a friend or a family member — or someone whom you actually want to use in an article. Develop a list of 10 interview questions, and then set up an interview with the person.

Questions:

    a.

    b.

    c.

    d.

    e.

    f.

    g.

    h.

    i.

    j.

✒ 11 ✒

Writing a Feature Article: Structure

WHAT YOU WILL LEARN IN THIS CHAPTER

• Feature articles must be organized clearly, so that they are understandable, logical, and easy to follow. Writers must pay close attention to an article's (1) theme, (2) unity, and (3) structure.

• An article must be unified around the theme, with all details relating to it.

• An article must flow smoothly from one point and one paragraph to the next.

• An article's structure includes three parts: the lead, body, and conclusion. The lead should be creative and attention-getting. The body uses either of two structures: narrative or thematic. The conclusion should "retell" in a creative way what the article was about.

*H*ave you ever sat down with a magazine, opened its pages, and found yourself quickly engrossed in one of its stories? You couldn't put the magazine down. You wanted to read every single word of the article.

On the other hand, have you ever sat down with a magazine and looked forward to reading one of the articles you saw promoted on the cover — but then were disappointed in how the article read? In fact, you didn't even finish reading the story.

If you had to describe a "really good" magazine article — like the first one mentioned — what would be some of its traits? What makes it satisfying to read?

On the other hand, what traits characterize a "bad" or ineffective article —

like the second one mentioned? Why doesn't it work?

You probably have an innate sense of why a magazine article is effective and interesting, or ineffective and difficult to read — even if you can't really give specific reasons why. You just know, as a reader, when the author has done a good job and crafted an effective piece.

It is important, though, for you as a writer to understand *why* some feature articles work and some don't. By understanding the characteristics of an effective article, you can incorporate those characteristics into your own articles.

The best articles have two primary characteristics. First, they are organized effectively, so that they are understandable, logical, and easy to follow. Second, they are enjoyable to read, because they have a certain sense of style achieved through various writing devices.

This chapter will tackle the first of these traits: the article's organization and structure. The next chapter will focus on the second, the article's style.

Let's start with the statement just used to describe a well structured article: *It is organized effectively so that it is understandable, logical, and easy to follow.*

How are such characteristics achieved? How does a writer organize material to create an effective article?

Writing a good article is where the rubber meets the road. It is at this stage that you take that great idea, add all the good information you've gathered, and put it all together in a final, polished piece that appeals to your reader. It's where you're faced with the challenge of organizing and structuring your idea, adding details, and putting together a coherent story.

To create an effective article, you must consider three points: (1) the article's theme, (2) its sense of unity, and (3) its structure.

The Article's Theme

At the very start, it's critical that you determine what the theme of your article is. Then you must assure that the article is built clearly around the theme. The theme is the main idea, the central point. Obviously, if you don't understand the theme before you begin writing, it is unlikely that you can focus the article on it. So a useful practice is to test yourself before you write down the first word of the article to see if you know the theme. A good way to conduct that test is to write the theme as one complete sentence before you begin writing the article. Keep it as simple as possible.

Here's an example. For an article on how to find a job during a slow economy, you might write your thematic statement like this:

"Finding a job during a depressed economy can be difficult, but several steps — keeping a current resumé, utilizing creative job-search resources, and being willing to embrace new opportunities — can help the process go more smoothly."

If you're unable to write the theme as one complete sentence, it means you don't yet know the theme. That can be frustrating. Don't, though, plunge into the article hoping that at some point you will discover the theme. You must think further about the theme until you know what it is. Only then should you begin writing the article.

Once you know the theme, keep it in mind as you write the article. Write it down on a piece of paper or on your computer where you can see it all the time as you work on your article.

The key to structuring an article effectively is to (1) have only one theme, (2) focus on that theme, and (3) stick to it. Be sure the theme is present in all parts — the lead, the body, and the conclusion (every single paragraph) — of the article. If you get sidetracked and your theme gets lost — and you begin writing about other topics that are only somewhat or vaguely related to the main idea — your story will lose its focus. Your confused reader will lose interest, and you will lose the reader.

The Article's Sense of Unity

To be effective, an article must have a sense of unity. Unity develops directly from the theme. We can thus think of it as *thematic unity*. You achieve unity by building your article around one clear theme. Every paragraph of your article must relate to that theme. In some way, each detail must be connected to the article's main idea.

An important device for creating a sense of unity is smooth transitions between paragraphs. You should never simply jump from one point to another point. Instead, take your reader logically through your article by using transitional phrases and statements that move seamlessly from one idea to the next. The essence of transition is that it connects each idea with the following one. Transitional devices include statements such as "On the other hand," "However," "At the same time," "Another thing to consider," "On the next day," and "You can also."

With many magazine articles — particularly how-to or informational pieces — you can provide a sense of transition with the use of subtitles, numbers, bullets, or other graphic elements to connect separate points. Such devices provide an easy way to move from one idea or point to the next. Don't, though, assume that they can take the place of real transitions in the flow of the writing.

Also important to the sense of smoothness is *paragraph unity*. This principle means that a paragraph must include one — and only one — idea. Don't group together unrelated sentences in the same paragraph. Each sentence should relate thematically to the paragraph's first sentence. A good practice is, after you write a paragraph, carefully read through it to assure that all sentences relate to the paragraph's main idea.

And don't, unless you have a specific reason to do so, write any one-sentence paragraphs. Be sure you adequately elaborate the idea in your paragraph — or more than one paragraph if you need more space to communicate the idea.

The Article's Structure

To craft a well-organized article, pay particular attention to the third element: your article's structure. Think of its structure as its layout, framework, or blueprint — the design that creates a complete and coherent account.

Every article has three parts: (1) a beginning, (2) a middle, and (3) an end. Magazine and newspaper writers normally refer to the parts as the (1) lead, (2) body, and (3) conclusion.

It's a simple structure. But a good feature writer thoughtfully considers each of the three parts. As you craft your article, you must determine how best to structure the beginning, middle, and end. The three must work together to create an effective whole.

Let's consider each of these parts and how to write them most effectively.

The Lead

The lead is a critical part of an article.

It also can be the most challenging part to write. So spend time with it. Gabriel Garcia Marquez, the Colombian novelist and short-story writer who won the Nobel Prize for literature, pointed out the importance of how one writes the beginning of a story. "One of the most difficult things is the first paragraph," he explained. "I have spent many months on a first paragraph, and once I get it, the rest just comes out very easily." That is a point worthwhile for feature writers.

The lead introduces readers to the topic, and it sets the tone for the rest of the story. If you do it right, the remainder of your article will come more easily for you.

The key in writing an effective lead is to introduce the topic and set the tone in a way that gets readers' attention and draws them into the article.

Many types of leads can do just that. They use creative techniques to interest readers. Instead of simply telling what an article is going to be about, good leads introduce the article in an entertaining way that will capture readers' attention and make them want to keep reading. Following are a dozen types of leads that feature writers typically use, with an example of each one. As you start writing feature articles, it is a good practice to consider this variety of leads. Then create one that works best for your specific article.

Notice from the following examples that leads vary in length. They may consist of one paragraph or an entire passage. The length is determined by the words necessary to achieve the purpose, but you should make your lead terse and direct. Eliminate unnecessary words. The length of the article also influences the maximum length of the lead. The longer the article, the more words the writer can allow for the lead.

---

1. *Summary Lead*

A summary lead — which is sometimes thought of as a straight news lead — states the key point of the article.

"Howard B. Unruh, 28, a mild, soft-spoken veteran of battles in Italy, France and Germany, killed 12 people with a war souvenir Luger pistol in his home block in East Camden Tuesday morning. He wounded four others."

2. *Direct Address Lead*

A direct address lead — a "you" lead — is calculated to involve readers personally in the article's topic.

"If you have a shape like a pear, don't let it bother you. You are more likely to succeed in life than most people."

3. *Anecdotal Lead*

An anecdotal lead tells a real-life story that illustrates the point of the article. While not always the case, anecdotal leads can be emotionally charged (poignant or humorous, for example).

"It's the night before Sarah's wedding. The images she'd dreamed of for years — the perfect dress, the meaningful vows, the sumptuous cake — now seem to reside only in the land of fairy tales. Her bridesmaids are fighting, her groom hasn't reported on the state of his vows, and the wrong flowers were ordered. Thinking of the disarray around her, Sarah bursts into tears. This isn't the way her wedding day is supposed to be."

4. Descriptive Lead

A descriptive lead describes a person, place, or event. It transports readers to the location or helps them "see" the setting of the subject the article will be about.

"The long line of khaki-clad youths stood at attention. The last notes of a bugle across the parade ground floated through the late-afternoon light. In the distance, a warm window light shone, and John Henry felt a lump growing in his throat."

5. Why Lead

A why lead emphasizes the "cause" and is combined with the "what."

"They told Williard Johnson he'd never be a football player. After all, he had only one leg."

6. Unbelievable Lead

An unbelievable lead grabs the reader's attention by revealing something startling. The reader will say, "I almost can't believe that," and then will want to continue reading to find out more.

"Five out of 100 people have an extra rib. Every three days a human stomach gets a new lining. The record for the loudest burp is 118 decibels, which is as loud as a chainsaw.

"'The human body,' says Dr. Sydney Faith, 'is not only amazing — but what it can do is surprising.'"

7. Cliché Lead

A cliché lead takes a familiar saying and puts a twist on it. The saying must be related to the theme of the article. Avoid bromides, platitudes, and triteness.

"A picture may be worth a thousand words, but it's not worth much of anything if it's out of focus."

8. Contrast Lead

A contrast lead combines two or more antithetic elements to make an idea more significant or interesting.

"School teachers went on strike this fall for the third time in eight years, but the city's 62,000 public school pupils were told to report to class."

9. *Quotation Lead*

A good quotation in the lead can draw readers into the article. The quotation, though, should be brief and part of the gist of the article. Don't use just any quote. Most importantly, the quote should be powerful.

"One evening in January when their children were in bed, Richard and Eugenia Smith sat before their television set, talking. 'All right,' Richard said coolly, in response to an accusation from his wife. 'I don't love you, I haven't for some time, and I want a divorce.'"

10. *Figurative Lead*

Metaphors, similes, and other figures of speech may be used in a lead. Be certain, though, to avoid triteness and banality.

"The colorful dark horse wearing a white rose, running headlong into the election of 1872, hoped to buck the 'superiority of man' harness off America's women."

11. *Question Lead*

A good question lead makes readers want to know the answer. Don't ask a frivolous question. Choose one that provokes your reader's curiosity.

"Were the best presidents of the United States the sickest ones?"

12. *Combination Lead*

Leads may combine two or more of the preceding types of leads. You might, for example, combine an anecdotal lead with a question lead. Such a lead would present readers with a real-life situation and then ask if they have ever been through a similar experience. Or you could combine a quotation lead with a direct address lead ... or you could use any other combination of lead types.

Whichever type of lead you decide to use, it's important to know the characteristics of a good lead. Make sure your lead is the best one possible for your article. The characteristics of a good lead are the following:

1. It is thematic, including important information that is germane to the story.
2. It is interesting.
3. It is slanted to the readership of the magazine.

There are also a number of pitfalls to avoid when writing leads. They can weaken your lead — and, in turn, the entire article. Be sure to follow these guidelines:

1. Never write a lead that does not relate to the theme of the article.
2. Never write a lead that says nothing substantive.
3. Never write a lead that does not relate directly to the interests of a magazine's target audience.
4. Never write a "cluttered" lead (too many facts and figures).
5. Never include unnecessary information in the lead.
6. Never present a false tone for the story that follows. Do not, for example, write a humorous lead for a serious story.

Most articles will follow the lead with a thematic statement that tells readers exactly what the point of the article is. This statement usually takes the form of a short paragraph. Writers often refer to it as the *nut graph*. Its purpose is to make clear to readers exactly what the article is about. Here is an example, taken from an article titled "Stalin Mystery Man Even to His Mother," written in 1930, which won the Pulitzer Prize for the author, H. R. Knickerbocker. The article is based on an interview with Josef Stalin's mother, who was disappointed that her son did not become a priest. The nut graph is the sixth paragraph.

TIFLIS, GEORGIA, USSR—A Georgian schoolboy was asked to name the foremost rulers in his country's history.

"Vachtang the Brave," he answered, "David the Restorer, Queen Tamara and Soso the Great."

"Why 'Soso the Great'?" asked his teacher.

"Because Soso was the first to annex Russia to Georgia."

The anecdote tells volumes, but not of course until one knows who Soso is. He is the ruler of 150,000,000 though his party calls him merely "the most trustworthy interpreter of Lenin's doctrines," and his title is only Secretary General of the Central Committee. His picture hangs in every shop, factory and office in the Soviet Union. It peers out from newspaper front pages at regular intervals all over the world. He is probably the most powerful political leader in any nation. In Russia his name is a cult, a promise and a threat.

It is none of these things to his mother. To Ekaterina Djugashvili, Joseph Djugashvili, known as Koba to the Czar's police, as Stalin to the world, is simply Soso, the son whose career, astounding, improbable, has not yet fully reconciled her to the disappointment she suffered when he failed to become a priest.

The Body

The body of the article is where you present all your information, make your points, and give your suggestions. It is where you reward your readers for continuing beyond the lead. It is where you give them the details promised in the lead.

As you construct the body of your article, it's your duty to make sure your article keeps on track. The central idea should be evident throughout all parts of the body of the article. The body should be unified and coherent.

Many articles lose steam about halfway through the body. The reader gets drawn away by an interesting commercial or television (at least more interesting than the article) or an enticing spouse (even if the lure is something as unexciting as washing dishes). Or the reader scratches his head and asks, "What does that have to do with anything?" Such responses probably mean one thing: The article lost its way somewhere along the way.

There are two primary designs you can use to construct your article in a unified and coherent way. These two forms — the narrative (or storytelling) approach and the topical (or thematic) approach — appear in magazines every day. Writers must learn the ins and outs of doing both of them.

The Narrative Approach

A narrative is a story. The narrative approach constructs the article in a storytelling fashion. It often is chronological, recounting the story as events took place, as a person's life occurred, or as a situation developed. It has a beginning and an end in time.

While the narrative approach doesn't work for some types of articles, it is natural for other types. You rarely see how-to articles, for example, written as a narrative. You might consider using a narrative structure for a personal experience essay (as you tell what happened to you in a chronological manner), a historical article (as you tell about a historical person or event as if it's a story), or a personality profile (as you present someone's life or story chronologically). The article "The Big Christmas Tree" on pages 207-210 in Chapter 14 is an example of a narrative story.

A narrative article typically uses the following structure:

1. Lead
2. Problem (situation) exists
3. Problem (situation) intensifies

Elaine Glusac
"Writing Travel Articles"

Q: Tell me a little bit about your experience getting started as a travel writer.

GLUSAC: I began freelancing in 1990, not long after completing grad school. I majored in history in undergrad and arts administration in graduate school as part of an MBA, both at the University of Michigan. Prior to writing, I worked in museums but felt my creativity was stunted. Freelancing, I found, allowed me to pursue my natural curiosity, a question-asking pattern that has bedeviled my mother from childhood.

I got my professional training on my feet, working for alternative and Italian newspapers in the Chicago area. But it wasn't long before I could quit the bartending job that paid the rent, and I began writing regularly for the feature pages of the *Chicago Tribune*. Though I wrote about fashion, fitness, health and women's issues, I gradually began writing more and more about travel, a lifelong passion. I have since written for most of the major travel publications and probably more of the lesser ones.

Q: What do you enjoy about travel writing?

GLUSAC: I'm basically excited about the topic. I could talk travel all day. At the same time, I think it's one of the hardest things to write, bringing an experience to life in a way that will engage the reader who really does not care about your vacation. I strive to make my stories relevant and picture my readers as people who don't have time to read my story, but, if I've been effective, they can't help themselves. Because it's hard, I enjoy it more, knowing that I will get better at it with each day of practice.

Q: What are the challenges in travel writing?

GLUSAC: The actual reporting requires juggling experiencing something and recording it, whether in notes, pictures or video. Too, the field reporting is expensive, and to make travel writing cost effective you have to do a lot in a little time. I read everything I can on a place before I go there so I am as familiar with it as I can be because I need to get my bearings quickly and start talking to people.

A good travel writer needs to be interested in everything — politics, art, music, food, architecture, transportation — and that's a lot of reading, listening, talking. The field reporting — the trips — is what most people focus on when they say they envy my job. But most of my time is spent at the desk, researching, writing, and interviewing.

Q: What are some of the writing techniques and style issues that are integral to writing good travel pieces?

GLUSAC: I really like voices, other than my own, in stories. I love quotes, and I don't think anything quite brings a place to life like hearing a local, even in print.

Travel writing, and probably all writing, requires an immediacy because no one is going to hang around while you develop a complicated or meandering lead. Get to it quickly and tell me why I should care. Stories still need a beginning, middle and an end, a dramatic hook that drives the pace. Lacking this is a common pitfall in travel writing.

Color is important. I think about immersing in the place: Is it hot? Am I sweating? Is the croissant still crispy but my hair curled by humidity? How can I work in these tiny details that say so much about a place while also moving the story forward? There's a tactile quality to good travel pieces that should stick to you like a T-shirt in the tropics.

Q: What insights might you give for students/writers who want to know how to better market themselves as travel writers?

GLUSAC: I think it's helpful to be well-rounded, to bring something besides your interest in travel to travel writing. It could be your perspective as an artist or art historian, a chef or avid cook, a hunter, a conservationist, a parent, a surfer, a Spanish speaker. Whatever your interests and skills are, they can find unique expression in travel writing. Expertise is becoming more and more important. Anything you can do to sharpen your skill set is key.

You also need to be smarter than your editors. The best way to get an assignment is to surprise someone with something they don't know. Drill deep and keep looking for leads. Become an expert in the field of travel. Know what's going on — from new museums and hotel openings, to where the latest outbreak of dengue fever is happening and what's the latest on travel restrictions to Cuba.

Q: What advice do you wish you had been told about travel writing earlier in your career?

GLUSAC: The business has to be something you love to warrant the effort. If not, there are much easier ways to make a living, even as a writer.

I made the mistake early on of thinking I could give magazines something better than they were publishing. But I've learned that publications like what they put out. While they may tweak and redesign, they want what they already have, especially in terms of voice. After reading loads of back issues, you should be able to intuit what a publication wants in a column, department or feature and then pitch yours in a way that is relevant to them. ✍

Elaine Glusac has written for most of the travel publications in print today. Her credits include the *New York Times, National Geographic Traveler, Conde Nast Traveler, Budget Travel, Islands, Men's Journal*, and many others. She can be found online at elaine glusac.com.

4. Problem (situation) is resolved

5. Conclusion: denouement, outcome, solution

The Topical (Thematic) Approach

Despite the narrative structure's usefulness for telling a story, most magazine articles use a topical approach. The reason is simply because it fits in so well with the type of topics and the easy-to-read approach most magazines take.

The topical approach takes the central idea and develops it according to secondary topics or points. All of these secondary points relate directly to the central idea and are often presented under a device such as a subhead. Subheads are smaller titles throughout the story. The phrase "The Topical (Thematic) Approach" at the beginning of this section is an example of a subhead. Secondary points can also be indicated with such devices as asterisks, bullets, other typographic elements, and numerals.

An article written with the topical structure typically is organized in the following manner:

1. Lead (which takes a creative, attention-grabbing approach to draw the reader into the story and suggest what the article will be about)

2. Thematic statement (a "nut graph," making it clear what the article is about)

3. Body of article

    a. Point 1 (elaborated with supporting material such as quotes, facts, observations, etc.)

    b. Point 2 (elaborated)

    c. Point 3 (elaborated)

    d. Other points as necessary

4. Conclusion (which ends the article on a satisfying note)

The Conclusion

Feature articles don't just end when they run out of material. They conclude with a proper wrap-up. They don't just stop when the writer runs out of words. Instead, they use obvious conclusions that sum up the main point or drive home the point in a way that is interesting and forceful. A good conclusion leaves readers feeling satisfied that the article is complete. The conclusion is the exclamation point on the article.

Feature writers have available many techniques for effective conclusions.

Articles can conclude with a strong summary statement, a poignant quote, a beautiful description, etc. Whatever device you use, though, try to conclude in a way that leaves your reader with a strong feeling.

In writing conclusions, pay particular attention to the following principles:

1. Make your conclusion relevant to the article's lead and the theme. The conclusion should tie the article together.

2. Plan your conclusion as an integral part of your article. Know what your conclusion will be before you even sit down to write the lead.

3. Look throughout your article to see if you have a quote, illustration, or some other material that would serve as a strong conclusion.

4. Be brief, pithy, and to the point.

Spend time with your conclusion. Read it several times. Then, if it needs a change, rewrite it as many times as necessary to get it right.

Just as there are principles to follow in writing conclusions, there are things you should avoid. They include the following:

1. Don't end without a conclusion. Don't just trail off.

2. Don't use a conclusion that ends weakly, falls flat, or has no impact.

3. Don't be repetitious, that is, simply restating phrases or specific points already in the article.

4. Don't be irrelevant, including material that is not pertinent to the article's theme.

5. Don't end on the wrong note, making a different point than is made in the article.

6. Don't use an ending that dilutes the point of the story.

7. Don't use an ending that leaves too much unresolved.

8. Don't sound contrived, trite, or inane.

9. Don't use an ending that preaches (thus jeopardizing the article's credibility by belaboring a point already made).

10. Be careful about using an ending that tells the reader what to think. The article's body should have given readers enough information to allow them to draw their own logical conclusion.

11. Don't be wordy or verbose, drawing out the conclusion longer than it should be. Say what needs to be said in an effective simple manner.

Several techniques work well in writing conclusions. Consider the following:

1. *Quotation*

Select a good quote from one of your sources and use it as a concluding thought. The quote should sum up the theme of the article.

Example: "Mathew Brady's legacy would make him proud, for he truly wanted to make his mark on history. In his own words, he felt an obligation as a photographer to 'preserve the faces of my country's historic men.' And he did."

2. *Description*

A descriptive scene at the end of your article will leave a specific image in the reader's mind. A description is especially effective if you started the article in a similar way, with a descriptive lead. This type of conclusion works especially well for personality profiles, personal experience pieces, and travel stories.

Example: "At the end of the day, the beach remains the most indelible image in our minds. The huge moon casts a magical glow on its bright, white expanse, and waves crash in the distance. It invites us to sit down once more, to hold hands once more while running our feet through its warm sand. It's what we will miss most about this island after we've left."

3. *Summary*

A summary conclusion reminds readers of what they have learned from your article. It summarizes the point of the article. It works well for an informational or how-to article because it keeps the facts foremost in the reader's mind.

Example: "Spending time in Europe after graduation can be an extremely rewarding experience. You will be exposed to a new culture, make new friends, expand your worldview, and be ready to tackle the future that awaits you back in the States."

4. *Circle*

A favorite way to approach conclusions, the circle technique connects the lead to the conclusion. It creates a "circle" from the beginning to the end of the article. The writer ties the beginning and end together by referring to the same idea in both. Sometimes, both use the same technique. For example, if the article begins with a quote from an expert in the lead, it uses another quote in the conclusion. Or if the lead asks a question, the conclusion restates the question and answers it.

Here's an example of the technique, taken from an article titled "10 Things I Learned as the Mom of a College Freshman." The lead refers to a "new parents" pamphlet that a college sends to the parents of freshmen attending orientation.

The article concludes with another reference to it.

The lead:

I'll never forget the day I came home from college orientation with my daughter and sat down to leisurely read the "Freshman Parents Survival Guide" pamphlet that the school gave to all the anxious mothers and fathers. I felt pretty confident that I could follow the guidelines (send care packages, trust your instincts, encourage her to get involved in activities) until I read that I "should not smother your child by talking to her every day. Consider calling or texting your child every two or three days."

Are they kidding me? I thought. They want me to talk to (or text!) McKenna every couple of days, when I'm used to talking with her many times over the course of a single day right now?"

The body of the article listed 10 things the author learned in the course of that freshman year.

The article concluded with a reference to the pamphlet mentioned in the lead:

Looking back on the day I first picked up that "Freshman Parents Survival Guide" (and anticipating McKenna's return to campus in mere days), I can truly say that she and I both changed more in nine months than we ever could have imagined. She is stronger and happier, our relationship is more mature, and she is headed in the right direction — and I truly believe that much of that comes from the conscious decisions I made to let her experience her freshman year in the healthiest, most effective, most independent way possible.

Spend time on your conclusion. Each part of your article is integral to its overall effectiveness. The conclusion deserves as much attention as any of the other parts.

Titles, Sidebars, and Other Extra Elements

The three main parts of the article structure are those we've just covered (the lead, body, and conclusion). Some other elements that writers provide, however, sometimes make it into publication along with the article text. They include the article's title, sidebars, and other extras.

1. *The Title*

The title for an article when it is published is usually written by the magazine's editor or other staff member. It rarely will be the title that you, the author, put on your article when you submitted it. It's still important, though, for you to come up with a good title and include it when you submit your article to the editor. On occasion, you may be surprised to find that a magazine did use your title — if it was catchy, appropriate to the style of the magazine, and interesting.

An effective title is one that captures the essence of the article's topic and is also interesting — one that will make the editor or readers want to read the story. Just as articles do, titles should be slanted at the interests of readers. Each magazine will have its own style for titles, and for a specific magazine you should put a title on your manuscript that is similar to titles the magazine uses. Here are some examples:

"Minding Your Parents' Business" (*Mature Living*)

"7 Things He's Not Telling You" (*Woman's Day*)

"Salad Bowls: Grow delicious fresh lettuce right in your own backyard" (*Southern Living*)

"The World's Dumbest Criminals, Celebrities, Lawsuits, and More" (*Reader's Digest*)

"Student Credit Cards That Make the Grade" (*Kiplinger's Personal Finance*)

2. *Sidebars*

Many articles include sidebars — "boxes" of supplementary information that go along with the main text of the article. Typical sidebars include items such as numbered lists, recommended readings, statistics, quotes, and additional resources. When you submit a query letter to an editor, go ahead and think of sidebar ideas to go along with your article and name them in your query. When your article comes out in print, sidebars will appear as boxes, charts, or other typographic designs.

Sidebars are popular in magazines and are especially useful to readers because they provide additional information in a way that is easy to grasp. They appeal to editors also and so are a great extra to include with your article.

3. *Other Elements*

Magazine articles can include other extra elements as well. Some of these items — which the magazine staff, and not the freelance writer, usually provides — include photographs, illustrations, and pull quotes (quotations set apart in boxes).

Spending proper time to consider how to put your article together is vitally important. Think through how each section will work, and then focus on making the article move along in a coherent way. Readers should always be able to follow your article logically. Don't lead them off on tangents. If you've structured the article correctly, the beginning, middle, and end will work together as a whole. The article's construction should be easy for readers to follow so that reading your article is a good experience. Once you understand article construction, writing articles will be a good experience for you, too.

Exercises

1. Read through several issues of a magazine and copy an example of each of the following types of leads:

    Summary lead

    Direct Address lead

    Anecdotal lead

    Descriptive lead

    Why lead

    Unbelievable lead

    Cliché lead

    Contrast lead

    Quotation lead

    Figurative lead

    Question lead

    Combination lead

2. Which three leads that you identified in Exercise 1 do you find most effective? Why?

    a.

    b.

    c.

3. Which three leads that you identified in Exercise 1 do you find least effective? Why?

   a.

   b.

   c.

4. Select a lead of one type that you identified in Exercise 1 and then rewrite it as a different type. For example, if you select a question lead, rewrite it as a why lead. If you select a direct address lead, rewrite it as an anecdotal lead.

5. Photocopy one lead from each of five magazines. Give the following information about each lead:

   a. Title of magazine:

   b. Title of article:

   c. Type of lead (question, narrative, etc.):

   d. Length of lead:

      (1) number of words:

      (2) number of sentences:

      (3) number of paragraphs:

   e. Theme of lead (what is the article going to be about?):

   f. How is the lead slanted to the magazine's readership? (Note such devices as subject matter, vocabulary, etc.):

6. Briefly (200-300 words) discuss the techniques of writing leads that you can learn from the leads in the previous exercise. What techniques, for example, do the leads use to capture the reader's interest?

7. Select two of the leads you identified in Exercise 5 that you think can be improved and rewrite them for the same magazines in which they appeared.

8. Select an article idea you have developed in a previous chapter of this book and write a lead for it.

9. Take the same article idea that you selected for Exercise 8 and outline how you would design the structure of the article's body.

10. Use the same article idea that you selected for Exercise 8 and list three sidebars to accompany it.

    a.

    b.

    c.

12

Writing a Feature Article: Outlining, Drafting, Revising

WHAT YOU WILL LEARN IN THIS CHAPTER

• Outlining organizes a writer's thoughts and information. The most common types of outlines are traditional, informal, and cluster outlines.

• Drafts of an article get the material organized. A writer may do any number of drafts.

• The polishing stage involves revising and improving an article to get it ready to send to a publication.

*T*he French writer Andre Gide once said, "Too often I wait for the sentence to finish taking shape in my mind before setting it down. It is better to seize it by the end that offers itself, head and foot, though not knowing the rest, then pull: the rest will follow along."

Although Gide was talking about novels, his sentiment is appropriate for feature writing as well. It is a useful way to think about getting started on writing a feature article. Writers sometimes wait for the "right" moment or the "right" sentence to get started writing, but waiting for such a creative urge suffocates the writing process.

To get an article started, it is best just to write something down.

In writing an article's first draft, your priority is simply to get words down on paper. Don't spend time polishing the sentences or hoping for just the right words to appear on your computer screen. Instead, be concerned with writing a draft that contains the main points you want to cover. Jacques Barzun, an American historian and an authority on style, cautions writers, "Convince yourself that you are working in clay, not marble, on paper, not eternal bronze: let that first sentence be as stupid as it wishes." When you start writing the draft, you may not know the exact words to communicate your main points. Your draft might even have gaping holes. But at least you're getting words on paper, and you're not stuck waiting for inspiration. "Writer's block" can be debilitating, and freelancers must not let it stop them.

Even before sitting down to write a draft, though, it's important that you take a number of preparatory steps. You need to plan what your finished article will be by outlining at the beginning of the writing stage. You must know where you're going before you start trying to get there.

Making an Outline

Once you've completed your research and collected all the information you need, you must decide how to use it within the structure of your article. The tool for the job is an *outline*. It will help you organize your thoughts before you actually sit down to write. Without an outline, you will be like the writer who throws himself willy-nilly into his first draft, without knowing where he's going.

The first step in creating an outline is to know what an article's central theme will be. The theme will serve as the organizing principle underlying the the article's entire structure. Knowing the theme will help immensely as you determine how to put together the parts of the article.

Feature writers take various approaches to outlines. Some use a formal outline following the Roman numeral style they learned in high school English class. Others use an informal outline. They put together a list of points that an article will include and write a brief phrase or two about each of them. Others like the cluster outline, which indicates points branching out from a central idea. Like the other two types, it's a good way to get the plan down on paper.

Whichever form you prefer, as long as you use some type of outline you will be a step ahead in the writing process.

The Formal Outline

The formal outline — the type that high school English teachers typically emphasize — organizes an article by main points and sub-points. If it were used for an article on, for example, taking the stress out of moving, it would look something like the following:

I. Lead: a quote from a mother who had difficulty when her family moved to another state

II. The stresses of moving
   A. Packing and unpacking
   B. Saying goodbye to friends and familiarity
   C. Making a new home

III. Dealing with stress
   A. Planning your move effectively
      1. Moving yourself
      2. Working with movers
      3. Giving yourself plenty of time
   B. Keeping the move simple and calm
   C. Getting comfortable with your new town

IV. Conclusion: a positive quotation from the mother quoted in the lead

You may be the type of writer who likes the specificity the formal outline offers. It works well for writers who like to plan every step along the way and who want to know they are not leaving out anything. If you use it, it definitely will help you get everything under control before you sit down to write.

The Informal Outline

Some writers prefer a more informal outline, one that simply lists in order the points they want to cover. You should not look at the informal outline as a way to avoid the rigor that organization requires. You still must think through your article thoroughly.

Here is how an informal outline might look for an article on consignment shopping:

1. Lead: an anecdote about two women's different shopping methods
2. Introduction of the main idea: After learning the basics of consignment shopping, you can save lots of money.
3. What are the benefits of consignment shopping? Include quotes from shop owners and shoppers.
4. Tips on how to be a good consignment shopper: Have a plan. Get to know the owners. Don't buy something just because it's cheap. Put your own clothes on consignment.
5. How to locate consignment shops in a town
6. Conclusion: Anecdote to tie in with the lead

While the informal outline is less structured than the traditional outline, it still accomplishes the same goal. The writer knows what's important and in what order the information will appear. Thus, the writer is equipped to start writing the article. It's also informal enough that the writer can easily alter the plan if necessary. The writer doesn't feel "locked in" to a formal outline. If the structure needs to be revised, it's easy to make the change.

The Cluster Outline

While the cluster outline is more popular with fiction writers and poets, it can also work for feature writers, especially those who plan and write in a free-style manner.

In using a cluster outline, you start with the central theme or idea of your article, which you write in a circle or box in the middle of your page. From that central topic, you branch off into corresponding ideas. You draw lines out from that circle/box into other circles that contain words or phrases that are next in line in your topic. Let's say the main topic is "Savannah, Georgia." Phrases in other circles connected to it would be such ideas as "historic squares," "quaint

Example of a Cluster Outline

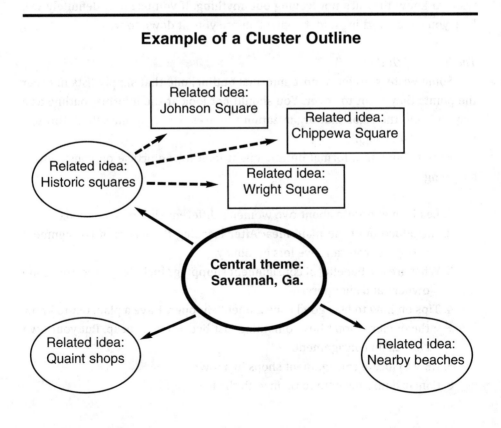

shops," and "nearby beaches." You keep drawing lines out to related sub-topics. From "historic squares," for example, you could make boxes for specific historic squares in Savannah.

The cluster outline allows you the freedom to add points easily. Not locking you into a formal arrangement, it also makes it easy to move ideas around.

The First Draft

Once you've outlined an article, it's time to tackle the first draft.

Remember this point about your first draft: It doesn't have to be perfect. The first draft is just that — a *draft*. It's a preliminary, first-stage writing of the article. It is not the finished product.

So don't feel you have to write a polished final manuscript. The draft may even have holes where you haven't written anything. Perhaps, in writing the draft, you discover that you need to get a quote from another source. In that case, you can leave an empty space and return to it later. The first draft is just the process of organizing your information. In later drafts, and then in the polishing stage, you can make your article "perfect."

As you work on your first draft, consider the following points:

• *Resist the temptation to edit or revise.*

As you write the draft, you might find yourself muttering things such as "That is so awkward ..." or "I really need to work on that ..." or "Ugh, that's not good at all...." You may be tempted to stop and correct each passage. Resist the urge, though. You will have time to revise and edit later. With the first draft, simply get all your information down on paper. Don't feel you need to perfect the writing.

• *Make broad notes about what needs work.*

Making notes about changes may sound like editing, but it's not. It just means you are aware at this stage of what parts need work, information you need to add, or passages that need rewording. Write notes to yourself in the margins, at the bottom of the page, or on Post-it notes — or type them within the computer text — about what you need to work on. You might, for example, say things like "Work on description here," or "Find another word," or "I need another quote on this point."

• *Realize that you probably can't complete the entire draft in one sitting.*

Most writers — both beginning and experienced ones — can't write a complete draft without interruption. In fact, it may take you several sittings. Give yourself plenty of time. Take a break if you need to. Don't put undue pressure on yourself or get tired from writing. When you do, you will see the result in flaws in your writing.

The Second Draft

How many drafts are required beyond the first one depends on the individual writer. Some writers do a first draft and just one more. Others go through three or four drafts. Once you begin writing feature articles, you will quickly learn what approach you need to take. However you handle drafts, your concern should be for quality and not for ease.

It's important to strike a balance between not doing enough work and doing too much. If you do little work on your first and subsequent drafts, the result probably will be a superficial article — one that will go unpublished.

On the other hand, if you do too many drafts, that might indicate that you are too attached to an article or too nervous about handing it over to other hands. Writers who are concerned about their work can understand this problem. They consider a piece of writing their "baby" — and some hold onto it dearly and want to make it perfect. They can feel as if they've never gotten it to a point where it's ready to submit to a publication. Keep in mind, though, that even though a feature article should be polished, you can't think of one article as your life's work. It is simply a short piece of writing. You need to finish it and move on to your next article.

The Polishing Process

Once you've finished the draft, your work has only just begun. It's time to get your article polished so that you can submit it to an editor. You need to determine how you can improve your article.

This polishing stage consists of four separate tasks: proofreading, editing, revising, and rewriting. They involve different types of work aimed at making your article better.

Proofreading

Proofreading involves examining the technical aspects of your article — its grammar, spelling, and punctuation. You must make sure you are following the rules that apply to each of those elements and that you are getting the mechanics as perfect as possible.

Most successful writers understand language mechanics. They know how to spell and use commas, and they understand subject-verb agreement. Their ability to use the language correctly improves their publishing success.

Many other writers have shortcomings with language mechanics. Some like writing but seem unaware of the rules, oblivious to the fact that the mechanical problems in their writing may mean that they never will succeed as freelancers.

Others know they sometimes make errors, and they want to improve. Using language mechanics correctly is not rocket science. One needs simply to apply oneself to the task. If you need help with grammar, spelling, or punctuation, take the following first steps to improve.

• Always use grammar and spell checks on your computer as a first course of action, but don't rely on them. Keep in mind that those programs have intrinsic problems. For example, many words that sound the same — such as right, rite, and write — are spelled differently.

• Invest in some good resources. Many books — such as those used in basic high school and college English composition courses — provide information on mechanical skills. Use them as guides to help you understand the rules.

• Find someone you trust to read your article. It could be a friend or family member, an acquaintance who is an English teacher, even a hired proofreader. If you have someone to proofread your work, you will have more confidence in the article you submit to a publication.

Editing and Revising

Editing and revising involve examining your article and working out the rough spots. Stephen King, the popular novelist, warned, "If you haven't marked up your manuscript a lot, you did a lazy job. Only God gets things right the first time." After you've corrected for grammar, spelling, and punctuation problems, read through the article and analyze how smoothly it reads and how clearly and interestingly it communicates its points. Consider such elements as organization, word choice, transitional phrasing, and effectiveness of quotes.

At the editing and revising stage, ask the following questions:

1. Have I left out any pertinent information?

**C.S. Sloan
"Writing for Specialized Magazines"**

QUESTION: Tell me about the type of specialty writing you do.

SLOAN: I write primarily for "bodybuilding" magazines — *Iron Man, MuscleMag International, Planet Muscle,* to name a few. Within that field — which is already specialized — I am known for "strength and power" articles. It's somewhat of a niche field.

Q: How did you get started as a freelance writer? And how did you get known as a writer who specializes in or is an expert in your area?

SLOAN: I got started when I was only 19. I grew up around a family of writers. So I was exposed to the elements of writing from a young age. However, to be honest, I didn't care much for writing. It was never really something that I tried to do, and it wasn't something that I was interested in doing. I was, though, very interested in bodybuilding. I was a voracious reader of all of the bodybuilding magazines. I would read every magazine that showed up on the magazine rack each and every month.

One day, I had sort of an epiphany. I had read so many articles on building muscle mass, and on gaining strength, that I realized: "Hey, I can write this stuff." So I wrote an article and sent it to two different bodybuilding magazines: *Iron Man* and *MuscleMag International.* (By the way, that's not something that you should do: send the same article at the same time to two different magazines.) Both of the magazines were interested in my material, but *Iron Man* accepted it first. So I had to write *MuscleMag* and tell them that I was sorry but *Iron Man* had already purchased it. Anyway, I was lucky because *MuscleMag* asked me for other articles.

A few years later, however, is when I started to get more articles in a variety of magazines, on the order of one every month. My first articles were generic bodybuilding articles, but when I started to write strength-specific articles — articles geared toward building as much strength as possible — my writing "career" took off. Few writers were doing

---

Look over your stacks of information and research (and also your outline) and ask yourself, Are there any facts that I forgot to put in?

2. Is my information accurate?

Never include inaccurate facts, or attribute a quote incorrectly, or spell someone's name wrong. Double-check every one of your facts at this stage of the article process even if you think you've got them right.

strength-specific stuff, and so the demand was higher.

Q: What is the advantage to specializing in a certain area, instead of writing about a lot of different topics?

SLOAN: As a writer, specialization really allows you to focus. The times when I wasn't very effective were the times when I tried to write different articles on topics other than body-building. Dabbling makes you a jack-of-all-trades, but a master of none, and not even a very good jack-of-all-trades at that.

Q: Is there a certain "style" of writing you have to use in your writing? Is style something that specialized writers particularly need to think about?

SLOAN: I think all writers have a certain natural "style" that they use. However, those who want to write for specialty magazines need to really understand each magazine that they write for. Study each magazine, read it all the time, and learn the "style" that the particular magazine wants. Substance should always be there, but style can change depending on the magazine.

Q: What advice would you give to someone who has an area of interest or expertise and wants to become a specialty writer?

SLOAN: If you truly love the area of interest, make sure you know everything there is to know about it. Just because you love it doesn't necessarily mean that you understand it. Also, make sure that it is something that you really enjoy. I have never written anything that I didn't want to write. If it isn't fun, if it doesn't make me smile, then I'm not going to do it.   ✍

C.S. Sloan is one of today's leading writers for magazines dealing with strength building. He is a contributing editor for *Planet Muscle* and *Iron Man* magazines and is a regular contributor to a variety of other print and online magazines. In 2011 *Planet Muscle* selected him as one of the top five strength writers in America.

---

3. Have I selected the best quotes?

Read the quotes you've used. Do they fit well with the rest of the article? Quotes should be used not just as fillers but as strong components of the story. Have you used them only when they are the best way to present the information? You should use direct quotes to present unusual or unique information that only the source can provide. Don't use a direct quote for information that could be easily obtained from observation, common knowledge, or any general source.

4. Does my article's organization make sense?

Answering this question should take a considerable amount of time. The editing, revising, and rewriting work related to your article's structure may be extensive. Your article *must* be well organized. A well-structured article contributes to a good reading experience. It allows a reader to go through an article without any abrupt stops or surprises. The reader senses that all the points logically relate to the central theme. Look through your article point by point. Do all of your quotations, anecdotes, facts — everything in your story — work together to give substance to the main topic? If not, eliminate an element or rewrite it until it does.

5. Are my transitions effective?

An article's flow depends on transitions. If an article has effective transitions between sentences, between paragraphs, and between sections, it won't have abrupt stops. The reader won't feel as if the article is bumping along from one sentence or paragraph to the next. If your paragraphs seem to exist in isolation from one another, readers will feel as if they're on a rough ride. The best way to eliminate the problem is to link paragraphs together both content-wise and stylistically. You can achieve that effect by repeating key words or phrases and by using transitional words or phrases — such as "Another way to ...," "However ...," or "You can also ..." — to link them.

6. Have I used words correctly?

Make sure all your words are the ones you meant to use. Double check for mistakes such as using "effect" for "affect," "set" for "sit," or "laid" for "lay." Be alert to connotations, for words that might present a different meaning to the reader than you had planned. Be precise. If you want to show that a person is "lurking" or "creeping" in the shadows, use one of those words instead of "walking" or "tip-toeing." Make sure your words convey the meaning you intend.

7. Will the meaning of all words and sentences be immediately clear to readers?

Feature writing must be clear. Stories must be easily understandable to the average reader. Magazine and newspaper readers — unlike readers of novels, or scientific reports, or poetry — will not stay with stories they can't easily comprehend. Feature writing that is not clear — that is not easily understood on a first reading — loses readers. You must avoid vague words, sentences, points, ideas, and logic. "Clarity. Clarity. Clarity," Strunk and White emphasize in *The Elements of Style.* "When you become hopelessly mired in a sentence, it is best to start fresh." Eliminate jargon, unclear words, and fancy phrases. Effective feature writing is direct. Its logic and meaning are plain.

8. Is my language economical?

Mark Twain said, "I never write 'metropolis' when I can get the same price for 'city.' I never write 'policeman' when I can say 'cop.'" Twain stressed economy of language in his writing. He knew what feature writers should remember: Long words, complex sentences, and a stilted vocabulary don't enrich writing but take away from it. You should use simple, strong words and sentences instead of complicated or indecipherable ones. Make sure your words are not obscure but clear and are suited to your readership. When a simple word or phrase will do, always go for the simple. Most readers of feature articles are reading to learn something or to be entertained — not to run to a dictionary to look up a word. Ernest Hemingway, the American novelist, explained his approach this way: "My aim is to put down on paper what I see and what I feel in the best and simplest way." Feature writers could do worse than to emulate Hemingway.

9. Is my language strong?

Just because your writing should be easy-to-understand doesn't mean that it can't be vibrant. Use vigorous words that communicate what you're trying to say. Judy Reeves, an author of books about writing, advises, "Audition your words.... Don't settle for red when crimson is the word you want." Use muscular verbs, strong description, vivid details, and accurate wording. Use language that transports your reader to a scene. Make your details as real as possible. Focus on your use of verbs. They are the most powerful words in the language. Take advantage of their power by using strong action verbs that convey precise meaning.

10. Can my style be strengthened?

The personal stamp you put on your writing is your style, and every writer's style is unique. Some writers have a conversational style, while others have a formal style. Your style sets your writing apart from that of other writers. It's what makes you the writer you are. As you write more and more, your style will develop. It will include such things as sentence structures, the tone of your writing, literary devices you tend to use, and how you handle descriptions. Charles Baudelaire, the French literary critic, advised, "Always be a poet, even in prose." As you edit your article, examine your style and see if you can strengthen it in any way.

11. Have I left out any necessary details?

Editing and Revising Checklist

As you answer each question below about an article you've written, circle YES or NO next to it. Make any comments to yourself in the space below the question.

YES   NO   Have I left out any pertinent information?

YES   NO   Is my information accurate?

YES   NO   Have I selected the best quotes?

YES   NO   Does my article's organization make sense?

YES   NO   Are my transitions effective?

YES   NO   Have I used words correctly?

YES   NO   Will the meaning of all words and sentences be clear to readers?

YES   NO   Is my language economical?

YES   NO   Is my language strong?

YES   NO   Can my style be strengthened?

YES   NO   Have I left out any necessary details?

YES   NO   Are my "extras" (sidebars, photographs, etc.) as good as they can be?

At the end of the editing process, do one final, thorough check of your piece. Make sure you've included all the information you need, assure there are no "gaps," and make sure you've left no questions unanswered. If there are gaps, go back and fill them in.

12. Are my "extras" (sidebars, photographs, etc.) as good as they can be?

Look at every aspect of your article — its title, photographs, sidebars, and anything else you're submitting — and make sure they are polished and complete. The *Writing Advantage* feature on page 182 provides an "Editing and Revising Checklist" in an easy-to-use form.

Rewriting

After you have proofread your article, and checked for various problems and missing elements through the editing and revising stage, you may find that you should rewrite some of your article.

This rewriting stage will involve such revisions as the following:

1. Adding information that was missing
2. Restructuring an order of points or information that doesn't flow logically or smoothly
3. Rewriting sentences or passages that, for any reason, are unclear

Most of the time, you probably won't find yourself doing major rewriting. By the time you get to a final draft, your article should be in good shape and will need only tweaking. Be willing, though, to rewrite when you need to. "Writing is rewriting," declared Richard North Patterson, an American novelist. "A writer must learn to deepen characters, trim writing, intensify scenes. To fall in love with the first draft to the point where one cannot change it is to greatly enhance the prospects of never publishing." Remember that you mustn't hold an article so close to the vest — or the heart — that you're unable to make changes that improve it.

Exercises

1. Edit each of the following sentences, paying particular attention to eliminating unnecessary words and using stronger verbs.

a. The reform movement reached its peak sometime between 1901 and 1912 and generally is considered to have ended with America's' entry into World War I in the year 1917.

    b. The reforms that were advocated covered a very wide range of problems and not all reformers agreed on every one of the reforms or their solutions, but their reform programs in general came to be known at the time as the Progressive movement.

    c. Although the movement had adherents in many different parts of the country, it was centered in the growing urban areas of America; and for the most part its backbone was composed generally of highly concerned middle-class, white-collar professionals.

2. Select an article idea that you developed earlier in this book, or choose another idea entirely. Write a one-sentence statement of the theme.

3. Create an outline (formal, informal, or cluster) for the article you selected in Exercise 2.

4. Taking the outline you created in the previous exercise, write a first draft of the article, concerning yourself only with getting words down on paper or the computer.

5. Let that first draft sit a day. Then write a second draft (and more drafts, if needed).

6. Let the article sit another day. Then, using the principles outlined in this chapter, edit and revise the article.

✍ 13 ✍

Writing a Feature Article: Style

WHAT YOU WILL LEARN IN THIS CHAPTER

• *Style* refers to the distinctive characteristics of a particular writer.

• Effective style can make writing enjoyable to read. Used poorly, style creates problems and repels readers.

• In developing a style that achieves maximum readability, a writer should avoid some techniques, ranging from wordiness to grammatical mistakes, and cultivate others, ranging from clarity to vitality.

Some writers just seem to have it.

They make readers sense a distinctive time and place. Or they serve up an interesting cast of characters and a compelling story.

Some make readers fall over laughing.

Some have a way with words and lines and rhyme, and their writing amazes readers with its simplicity and, yet, with its depth.

One of today's most popular nonfiction authors is Rick Bragg. He writes about his family and his heritage in best-selling memoirs. His Pulitzer Prize-winning articles take readers to places far and wide and teach them timeless lessons. Even his stories of sports evoke something inside many readers that is usually reserved for love or faith. He is featured in the "Writer Spotlight" on pages 196-197 in this chapter.

What makes his writing so good is not just the topics he chooses. It is his use of phrases, images, details ... his language. It is, simply put, his style. His readers say he just has a "way with words."

185

You can probably understand what they are talking about. Think about your own favorite authors and ask yourself why you love them. Chances are you like the stories they tell — but you also like the way they tell those stories.

It's their style that really matters.

The Importance of Style

What, exactly, is *style*?

The term is used in a number of ways. In this chapter we are referring to the distinctive marks of a particular writer — the techniques that make his writing good and enjoyable to read.

Your style is what makes your writing unique ... what makes you "you." Effective style, though, is not self-indulgent. It does not point to itself or try to show off what you can do with your writing.

The poet and novelist Wallace Stegner discussed style in an article titled "To a Young Writer" in *The Atlantic Monthly* back in 1959. In explaining why he thought the writer had been successful, he wrote:

"For one thing, you never took writing to mean self-expression, which means self-indulgence. You understood from the beginning that writing is done with words and sentences, and you spent hundreds of hours educating your ear, writing and rewriting until you began to handle words in combination as naturally as one changes tones with the tongue and lips in whistling." The problem with many young writers is that they will not conform to the accepted standards of writing. They "have only themselves to say and ... are bent upon saying it without concessions to the English language." However, anyone "who sets out to use [language] expertly has no alternative but to learn it."

The key, Stegner is saying, is that good writing requires the writer to be concerned foremost about the use of language, not about himself. A good writer is not one who wants to show how fancy he can be with words.

Other successful writers make the same point. For example, consider the following observations:

Ralph Keyes, American non-fiction book author: "Confident writers have the courage to speak plainly: to let their thoughts shine rather than their vocabulary."

Jorge Luis Borges, Argentine poet and essayist: "At the beginning of their careers many writers have a need to overwrite. They choose carefully turned-out phrases; they want to impress their readers with their large vocabularies. By the excesses of their language, these young men and women try to hide their sense of inexperience. With maturity the writer becomes more secure in his ideas. He finds his real tone and develops a simple and effective style."

Good writing seems natural when we read it, but it actually takes great discipline to achieve. It seems so easy, and yet the reader, on reflection, knows that the writer worked hard at it. To be a good writer, you must become a student of your style. You must learn the rules of the English language. You must study what works and doesn't work. Yet, your writing needs to come across as natural.

Does that seem impossible?

Perhaps. But it's not. It simply takes work — as everything that is worth anything does. Once you have mastered language, it will seem easy to use.

Those who want to succeed as feature writers must spend time developing their style. Although a writer may find himself saying, "I don't have a style. That's something for the Faulkners and Hemingways and Austens of the world," everyone who writes anything does have a style. It may be polished or awkward, but no matter what its quality is, the style is important.

Problems To Eliminate

Good feature articles have characteristics — such as strong descriptions and vigorous language — that set them apart from ordinary ones. Commonplace writing is marked by its own characteristics — such as wordiness, redundancies, vagueness, and clichés. You need to eliminate the problems and cultivate the effective techniques. To help with that task, let's first consider some common problems that plague writing.

Ostentatious Words

Some people are proud of their large vocabularies, but a feature article is not the place to put big words on display. Don't be tempted to use long or complex words. They are unnecessary and will create a roadblock to readers, discouraging them from reading the rest of the story. The novelist Stephen King advised, "Any word you have to hunt for in a thesaurus is the wrong word. There are no exceptions to this rule."

Clichés

Phrases such as "busy as a bee" and "a picture paints a thousand words" may seem comfortable to us, but just because we use them in our routine conversations doesn't mean we should use them in our writing. There's no rule that says clichés may never be used. They are okay on occasion but only if they are appropriate and strong. If a phrase sounds too familiar, don't use it. Instead, come up with a creative way to say the same thing in a different, special way.

Jargon

Particular groups, trades, and professions use language that is peculiar to themselves. That language is known as jargon. Scientists and lawyers, for example, have a jargon all their own, and it's different from a housewife's. Feature articles should use language with which readers are familiar. Jargon will come across as stilted, and the average reader may have difficulty understanding it.

Vagueness

Make details and facts as precise as possible. "The man owns a lot of cars" is indefinite compared to "The man collected 30 vintage cars and motorcycles." Vagueness will lose readers. You will keep them interested if your information and wording are concrete and strong.

Overuse of Adjectives, Adverbs, and "Fancy" Figures of Speech

New writers often go overboard in their use of description, leaning too highly on adjectives, adverbs, similes, allusions, and the like. The strongest word in the English language is the verb because it connotes action. Next is the noun. It puts the who or what into the action.

Adjectives and adverbs can add detail and description, but they can also be superfluous. Anton Chekhov, the Russian short story writer and playwright, advised, "Cross out as many adjectives and adverbs as you can.... It is comprehensible when I write: 'The man sat on the grass,' because it is clear and does not detain one's attention. On the other hand, it is difficult to figure out and hard on the brain if I write: 'The tall, narrow-chested man of medium height and with a red beard sat down on the green grass that had already been trampled down by the pedestrians, sat down silently, looking around timidly and fearfully.' The brain can't grasp all that at once, and [writing] must be grasped at once, instantaneously."

Read your article and ask yourself if you have chosen the best words. Pay careful attention to adjectives and adverbs by circling them and then making sure they are necessary.

Careless Spelling

Misspelled words are among the most noticeable of all mistakes in print. They stick out like a *swore* thumb and make you look like a careless, unprofessional writer. Be diligent in making sure words are spelled correctly. If you have any doubt about a word, look it up in a dictionary. If it's a word that has alternate spellings, look it up in the dictionary. And if you know you have trouble with spelling, invest in a dictionary and keep it near you at all times.

Careless Word Use

Writers should never use a word incorrectly. Some words, though, cause more problems than others. Be sure you're aware of them. Some of the most commonly misused words are the following:

Accept / Except
Affect / Effect
Allusion / Illusion
Can / May
Capital / Capitol
I / Me / Myself
Its / It's
Lay / Lie
Less / Fewer
Principal / Principle
Set / Sit
Than / Then
There / Their / They're
Who / Whom / Which / That
Your / You're

Keep a dictionary handy so you can double check any words you may be confused about. Be sure to use them correctly.

Switched Tenses

Every piece of writing has a tense. Things happen (in the present tense) or happened (in the past tense). As you write, keep the tense in mind. Don't get confused and hop back and forth between tenses. Find out if the magazine you are writing for has a preferred tense. If it doesn't, simply decide on a tense ("says" or "said") and stick with it throughout your article.

Passive Construction

The passive voice puts the emphasis on the results of an action rather than on the action itself. It focuses on the *recipient* of the action, rather than the *performer* of the action. Therefore, the passive voice lacks the power of the active voice.

Compare the following sentences:

"The expectant wife was driven to the hospital by her frantic husband."

"The frantic husband drove his expectant wife to the hospital."

The second sentence is more effective because it communicates a sense of action. Someone is *doing* something. The first, on the other hand, slows down the action. Someone is having something done to her. A sure indicator that a passive construction is weak is when it incorporates the word "by" — as in "by her frantic husband." A good practice is to do a search for the word "by" in a manuscript and to rewrite any sentence that uses it with a passive verb.

Exclamation Points

Most of us speak in exclamation points, and most of us fill casual correspondence — such as emails, tweets, and text messages — with them. You can write an entire magazine article, however, and never need an exclamation point. Some writers use exclamation points inappropriately when a period is all that's really needed. If you feel you must use an exclamation mark, that probably means that you've not chosen the right words to make your point as emphatically as you should. An exclamation point can be a sign of amateurism. Use it sparingly and only in situations where it absolutely is needed. F. Scott Fitzgerald, the American novelist and short story writer, advised, "Cut out all those exclamation marks. An exclamation mark is like laughing at your own joke."

Other Personal Punctuation Favorites

Most writers lean on their own personal favorite punctuation marks and overuse them. I really like hyphens, dashes, semicolons, and parentheses — can't you tell? So I have to be careful not to overuse them. In fact, I went through the manuscript for this book, checking for such punctuation marks, and, believe it or not, removed a huge number of them. Used too much, they become noticeable and hinder the reader. In most sentences, semicolons are unnecessary, and a sentence using them can be rewritten as two sentences. Make sure you use question marks, semicolons, parentheses, hyphens, asterisks, ellipses, and so forth only in the way they are intended to be used — and use them sparingly.

Common Grammatical Mistakes

The English language can quickly overwhelm you. Many of its rules of grammar seem arbitrary. Some don't even seem to make sense. And, yes, there may be entirely too many of them. It's still important, though, that you become a master

 **Books on the Craft of Writing**

The following books are excellent resources to guide you toward becoming a better craftsman of language. Some are considered "classics," while others probably are on their way to becoming classics.

> *On Writing Well* by William Zinsser
> *The Elements of Style* by William J. Strunk Jr. and E. B. White
> *The Chicago Manual of Style*
> *The AP Style Book*
> *Reference Handbook of Grammar and Usage* by Porter Gale Perrin
> *Writing with Power* by Peter Elbow
> *On Writing* by Stephen King
> *Bird by Bird* by Annie Lamott
> *Zen in the Art of Writing* by Ray Bradbury

---

of the language — whether that includes spelling, punctuation, or grammatical rules. You need to understand subject and verb agreement, the proper use of "who" and "whom," dangling participles, and the many other terms and rules that reveal your professionalism and mastery as a writer.

There are more rules than we can discuss here, but you probably have a sense of whether you need to work on them or not. You should know if grammar is one of your problem areas. Failure to follow grammatical rules will limit your publishing success.

Besides studying proper language, the best weapon with which you can equip yourself is a good book on grammar. Study the rules in it, read it often to refresh yourself, and use it as a guidebook whenever you have a specific question or problem with a word or sentence. Classics such as *The Elements of Style* by Strunk and White or *The Chicago Manual of Style* are excellent resources for feature writers.

The *Writing Advantage* feature "Books on the Craft of Writing" on this page provides a list of recommended books to help you with the use of language.

Another good way to eliminate problems is to find a reader/editor who is skilled in language mechanics. Find a friend or family member who is good at grammar, or hire an editor who can give your article the "once over" in grammar,

Problem Area Checklist

This checklist will help you remember those problems you need to avoid in your writing. Your goal should be to write a clean, readable article. By familiarizing yourself with these problem areas, you can noticeably improve your style.

Are any of the following elements evident in your article?

_____ Wordiness

_____ Clichés

_____ Jargon

_____ Vagueness

_____ Overuse of adjectives or adverbs

_____ Spelling errors

_____ Careless word use

_____ Switched tenses

_____ Passive construction

_____ Overuse of exclamation points and other punctuation marks

_____ Grammatical mistakes

---

punctuation, and spelling areas.

As you prepare to write your feature article, be particularly aware of potential language problems. Realize that the more you write, the more natural your writing will become and the less these avoidable problems will crop up. Writing — and especially writing well — is a process. Your style, as well as your comfort level with writing, will develop exponentially the more you write.

See the *Writing Advantage* feature on this page for a checklist of problems.

Techniques To Cultivate

Just as there are things to avoid in developing a strong writing style, there are also techniques to cultivate. The following techniques will make your writing stronger, more precise, and more interesting and readable:

Substance

Your writing should be substantial. Provide enough information and details for the reader to understand the topic. Fill out an article with complete facts, descriptions, anecdotes, examples, quotes, and other elements. The most important ingredient in good writing is good material.

Vitality

Give color and life to your writing with characterization, details of setting, dialogue, story, color, strong words ... all of those things that make writing rich and nuanced. "Details, truthfully rendered," says Judy Reeves, a writing teacher and author of books about writing, "bring your writing to life and create connection points for the reader."

Attention to Word Choice

The word is the writer's basic tool. Just as an electrician knows which tool to use for which job, or a golfer knows which club to use for which stroke, the writer needs to know which words to use for which purpose. George Orwell, the British novelist and critic, declared, "A scrupulous writer, in every sentence that he writes, will ask himself at least four questions, thus: 1. What am I trying to say? 2. What words will express it? 3. What image or idiom will make it clearer? 4. Is this image fresh enough to have an effect?"

Never haphazardly throw words onto a page, but instead think about how to use the words. In *The Elements of Style*, William Strunk, Jr., advises, "A sentence should contain no unnecessary words, a paragraph no unnecessary sentences, for the same reason that a drawing should have no unnecessary lines and a machine no unnecessary parts." Use the right words to convey the correct meaning. Make sure your words flow well and that you are using precise, uncluttered, vivid words.

Effective Anecdotes

Anecdotes are stories that serve as examples, and they are important in feature articles. They add life.

Feature articles can use anecdotes in two primary ways. Anecdotes can help the reader identify with the topic by providing a story about familiar people or situations. They can also be used to clarify or accentuate a point.

The primary reason you use anecdotes is that they involve people — and remember that people (characters) pull in readers more than anything else. Readers want to hear about people like themselves, or people fascinating to them, or people they would like to emulate. People involved in situations and stories add drama, color, and reality to articles in a way that few other things can. By telling readers about people who are similar to them, articles immediately draw readers into the story and make them more interested in the topic.

Here, as an example, is a lead that uses three anecdotes to introduce an article on starting family holiday traditions:

> Every Christmas Eve, Brad and Caroline practice the same ritual with their five-year-old daughter, Caitlin. They cuddle up in front of the fireplace, read "Twas the Night Before Christmas" together, and drink Caroline's homemade peppermint cocoa.
>
> When all the Hanukah festivities are over, Matthew and Joanna sit down with their children and relive a tradition every year. Sons Tucker and Derek and daughter Lauren each pick one favorite memento from the holiday (a photo from a family gathering, a bow from a favorite present, and so forth) and place it in their family Hanukah Box. They found the trunk at a thrift store and decorated it with wrapping paper when Tucker was barely a year old.
>
> Single mother Tricia and daughter Quinn also have a special Christmas tradition. They spend a Saturday evening a few weeks before every Christmas making a homemade tree ornament together. Their tree now has 15 homemade ornaments, each with a specific, special memory behind it.

Quality Quotes

Readers not only like to read about people, but they also like to hear them talk. Quotation marks around words make them seem alive. Something is going on. People are talking. "Most readers," explains writer Phyllis Whitney, "prefer to find lots of conversation in the stories they read. A solid page of print, unbroken by dialogue, is tiresome to the eye."

So sprinkle your writing with good, pungent quotes. The quotes should be powerful and interesting. They should be appropriate to the topic. They should provide concrete information that readers can't get from another source. They should move the story along. And they should reveal personality and emotion.

When, for example, I was given the following quote while working on an article about a tornado survivor, I knew I had to use it: "We all know that if it weren't for that whole community working together, he would have bled to death. And that's just a miracle." The quote was too powerful not to use. In fact, it became the conclusion of the story.

Remember, though, that too much of a good thing is always a hazard. Don't rely so heavily on quotes that they become the structure of the article. Article writing is not the same as stenography. Be careful in the quotes you select, and don't go overboard.

"Show; Don't Tell"

The old adage "Show; don't tell" is a good one to remember as you write feature articles. It brings vitality to your characters, environment, theme, and story.

Instead of simply saying that a person is sad, frightened, angry, or pleasant, *show* that she is. Include details — such as quotations, actions, dress, or appearance — that identify those characteristics.

Instead of saying that a place is ugly or pretty, show that it is. Describe the scene, and involve people in it who reveal its character. For example, instead of writing, "The city needed repairs everywhere," write something like, "The city showed its age like an old actress. Its dirty streets, crumbling buildings, and graffiti-filled walls revealed nothing of the grand woman she used to be. A man in a worn shirt mumbled that he was tired just from living in the city."

Mechanical Correctness

Good grammar, proper punctuation, and correct spelling are all signs of a professional writer. Improper mechanics are sure to turn off readers — that is, in the unlikely event that the article ever gets into print.

Pay attention to the technical aspects of your writing. Analyze it closely and eliminate all mechanical errors. Be sure grammar, spelling, and punctuation are correct.

Write a draft. Then rewrite. After you've rewritten, read and edit the second version critically. Correct and polish the writing as you write a third version.

Literary devices

You may think that literary techniques such as similes, metaphors, allusions, and alliterations can be used only in poetry or fiction. Appropriately used, though, they can add interest and style to nonfiction articles.

Metaphors refer to something familiar in order to clarify or improve an image. They compare one thing to another in a way readers will understand. Shakespeare, for example, used two metaphors in the following familiar line: "All the world's a stage, and all the men and women merely players."

A *simile* is similar to a metaphor in that both clarify an image by comparing it to another image, but a simile uses the word "like" or "as." Here are some exam-

Rick Bragg
"Nonfiction Writing Style"

Q: If you were making a list of the characteristics of effective feature writing style, what would they be?

BRAGG: To me there is really only one, and that is an old journalism boilerplate called "show me; don't tell me." You have to think scenes. You have to put people where you are. You have to create through your writing an event, or a happening, or a conversation that not only sums up your story but gives people almost a story within a story. If you paint a scene, if you show rather than tell, if you use color and imagery and detail, then you win.

Q: In your own feature writing, what characteristics do you pay particular attention to (such as description, setting, or word choice)?

BRAGG: The description, of course, because if you don't give your readers flavor then it's just like feeding them food with no seasoning. My mother once said of a bland cook, "She is afraid of the salt shaker." A writer can't be afraid of the salt shaker. In feature writing, you have to give it flavor.

I like pointed words, short words. I don't like passive words. I like unusual words. Instead of saying that someone who has suffered a long-term injury is "injured," I might say that he is "damaged." Think of the unusual word, but it has to fit. Word choice can be everything.

Q: How would you describe your own writing style?

BRAGG: The nicest thing anybody ever said about me was what Maureen Dowd [the syndicated columnist] once said: that I write in color. I hope I can make a scene come alive. I work real, real hard at it. I like to think that I can write clearly. But one thing I try to avoid more than anything else is melodrama, gothic silliness. Instead, I just go for the big and rich, simple detail.

---

ples from nonfiction writing. They are taken from stories in the book *Masterpieces of Reporting* (Sloan and Wray, editors). You will notice that each author characterizes a detail in a way that helps the reader to visualize it more clearly.

"In the hollow of the ridges the mist lay like broad lakes of water, and on one side of the plain stood the walls of the old town. On the other rose hills cov-

Q: How can nonfiction feature writers incorporate more literary devices into their writing (devices more often seen in fiction writing)?

BRAGG: The writer needs to remind himself not to be afraid. Nonfiction writers are often afraid of the literary sense. That is just foolish. As an old baseball coach I had once said, "Just rear back and hum it." That does not mean that you over-write.

What it means is, write the pretty sentence. At Timothy McVeigh's trial, after the Oklahoma City bombing [in 1995], I had no fancy writing in the lead of my story, but I think it was one of the best I ever had. It was, "After the explosion, people learned to write left-handed, to tie just one shoe. They learned to endure the pieces of metal and glass embedded in their flesh, to smile with faces that made them want to cry, to cry with glass eyes. They learned, in homes where children had played, to stand the quiet. They learned to sleep with pills, to sleep alone."

There's not one "fancy" line in that. It's just images — but I hope it reads more like literature than it reads like a cop brief or like a city council meeting.

Q: What advice would you give to aspiring writers who not only want to get published or make money from their writing, but who want to be known for good writing style?

BRAGG: Volunteer for the hard stuff, for the stories of human suffering, of sadness, of loss. Those stories, because of tone and content, are always going to be taken seriously. Those serious stories will force you to be a better writer. They will force you to write with that color, with that imagery and detail. They will get more attention.

Oddly enough, it's not the craft that will make your reputation a lot of times, but the content. If you seek out serious stories, then you will have to write seriously about them — but not in a dull, plodding way. You'll have to write with power and grace and color to do them justice.

Rick Bragg is a prize-winning writer and bestselling book author. He won the 1996 Pulitzer Prize for feature writing at the *New York Times*, authored such acclaimed books as *All Over But the Shoutin'* (Random House, 1999; based on his years growing up in Alabama), writes for a variety of national magazines, and is well-known for his stylistic nonfiction writing.

---

ered with royal palms that showed white in the moonlight, like hundreds of marble columns." — Richard Harding Davis, "The Execution of Rodriquez"

"There was a muffled noise like the slamming of some large door at a good distance away." — Floyd Gibbons, "German U-Boat Sinks Laconia"

"Darkness like a blanket wrapped the alleyway and the box-like old prison."
— Royce Brier, "Murderers Meet Violent Death at Hands of Mob"

"By this time the sky became so full of flak, tracers, shell bursts, and spotlight streaks that it was like the fireworks at the county fair." — Robert E. Bunnelle, "The Bombing of Cologne"

"She hugs and hugs, hanging on, happily. Her stomach, looking like a volleyball, peeks out of her black dress. It quivers some. Then the woman purrs, like the cat she alternately pets and paddles." — Margo Huston, "I'll Never Leave My Home. Would You?"

Here are some other literary devices you might want to consider using:

Alliteration, using repetition of sounds: "The cherry tree strews petals on the green lawn of his grave."

Internal rhyme, using rhyme within a sentence or phrase: "His flame of criminal fame was extinguished after a short career, and he spent the next six years in the grim, dim confinement of a New Jersey prison."

Allusion, referring to something such as history, mythology, literature, pop culture, or religion with which the reader is familiar: "Like the prodigal son, he spent years looking for pleasure — but found no satisfaction."

Personification, giving a personality to something inanimate: "What should be sad in the falling of spent leaves, of leaves that have decked themselves in bridal hues to keep a tryst with death? The leaves are glad enough. They spiral down from their parent twigs to carpet the loam. If a wind drives over them, they blithely dance in the hazy sunshine of autumn."

Clarity

Be clear. Matthew Arnold, the English poet, emphasized, "Have something to say and say it as clearly as you can. That is the only secret of style." Especially in newspaper and magazine writing, clarity may be the most important feature. Christopher Morley, an American journalist and essayist, declared, "The three chief qualities of style are clearness, force and ease.... [T]he rule of clearness is not to write so that the reader can understand, but so that he cannot possibly misunderstand." Remember that feature writers are writing for the benefit of the reader. Don't leave questions unanswered. Identify each person in an article. Identify or locate place names. Don't make seemingly contradictory statements without clarification. Be consistent throughout your story.

Personal Style

Style is personal. It's created by the likes and dislikes of the individual writer, and it comes naturally the more you write.

Feature writers can use creative license to do such things as write sentence fragments to express urgency or write in a stream-of-consciousness to recreate someone's thoughts. Remember, though, that you should not create a unique style just to do it. You shouldn't draw attention to yourself. Creative license should be used only when it is better than a traditional method — when it's done for a particular purpose.

The best way to learn how to write well is to read good writing. If you are serious about becoming a successful feature writer, you should immerse yourself in reading good short nonfiction articles. The *Writing Advantage* feature "Collections of Feature Articles" on page 200 provides a list of books and websites where you can locate excellent examples of nonfiction work.

The Bottom Line on Style

Developing an effective personal style — writing in a way that says, "That sounds like something Ima Riter would write" — will make your articles shine in a way that will win and keep readers. Beware, though, of the tendency to overdo it. Your writing should be entertaining to read, but that doesn't mean it should be so dramatic or colorful that it draws attention to itself. If it does, it will draw the reader away from the story.

As you examine your writing, consider these two questions: "Is my article readable?" and "Did I try too hard?"

Is my article readable?

Your reader must get something out of your article. The message must not get lost inside an opaque presentation.

To determine if your article is readable, first try to read it with an objective eye. Read it aloud, record it, and play it back, or have someone else read it to you. Listen for any problem spots: unnecessary words, vague information, clichés, choppy transitions, passive writing, and other details that just don't feel "right."

Then ask a writer friend, or a friend who has an interest in your topic, to read the article and ask her: Is the main point of the story clear? If it's not, then the central idea has gotten lost somewhere, and you need to restructure the article.

 Collections of Feature Articles

To be a good feature writer it is important to read good feature writing. The following books and websites provide excellent examples of nonfiction writing.

http://www.pulitzer.org/bycat/Feature-Writing
The online site of the Pulitzer Prize provides full texts of all winning feature articles. Some categories other than "Feature Writing" — such as "Explanatory Journalism" and "Investigative Reporting" — also contain feature-style stories.

The Art of Fact: A Historical Anthology of Literary Journalism, Kevin Karrane (ed.)

The Best American Magazine Writing, American Society of Magazine Editors (eds.), an anthology published annually

The Best of Creative Nonfiction, Lee Gutkind (ed.), an anthology published annually

The Best of Pulitzer Prize News Writing, Wm. David Sloan, et al (eds.). Despite the title, most of the articles in this anthology are long-form stories such as personality profiles and narratives.

Masterpieces of Reporting, Wm. David Sloan and Cheryl S. Wray (eds.). Most of the articles in this anthology are long-form stories.

The following sources provide excellent tips on writing effective nonfiction.

www.brevity.wordpress.com
The blog home of *Brevity: The Journal of Concise Nonfiction*

www.creativenonfiction.org
The online version of the print magazine *Creative Nonfiction*

Telling True Stories: A Nonfiction Writers' Guide from the Neiman Foundation at Harvard University, Mark Kramer (ed.)

Did I try too hard?

In developing a personal style, new writers often go overboard. While trying to sound creative, they end up sounding amateurish. They put in too many descriptions, or load down the writing with artsy words, or throw in too many literary devices.

Remember: A little bit goes a long way. Anecdotes won't work at all if they're not balanced with good, solid information. Similes won't work if you put them in every paragraph. By practicing restraint, you will learn where the techniques are really needed.

Above all else, your story must be readable and interesting. You can accomplish that by avoiding the blunders of bad writing and cultivating the techniques that work.

Exercises

1. What does "style" mean to you? Define it with a one-sentence statement. Write a one-page essay on the term's meaning to you.

2. Select a short article (preferably, a one-page article) published in a magazine, and edit it closely for (a) mechanical correctness, (b) clarity of wording, and (c) use of verbs. As you edit, try to improve the wording.

3. Using the article that you read for Exercise 2, identify the techniques the writer used that made the article's style effective? Make a list of those techniques.

   a.

   b.

   c.

   d.

   e.

4. Using the article that you read for Exercise 2, select five sentences from the article and rewrite them to make them more effective.

   a.

   b.

   c.

   d.

   e.

5. For each of the following article topics, write an anecdote that illustrates the topic. For this exercise, you may create imaginary scenarios.

    a. How to unstop a drain

    b. A profile of a cancer survivor

    c. An analysis of paying for a college education

    d. Ways to celebrate Thanksgiving

    e. What it means to be "in love"

6. For each of the following situations, using your observational skills and imagination, write a description of 100 to 150 words. Include concrete details.

   a. A thunderstorm

   b. The best vacation you ever had

   c. Your last conversation with your mother

   d. A doctor's office

   e. The location you are at right now studying this book

7. Read one feature article that has won the Pulitzer Prize. You can find the winning articles at this website: http://www.pulitzer.org/bycat/Feature-Writing.

a. Title of article:

b. List three examples of good word choice that the writer uses in the article. Explain why the wording works well.

c. How does the writer create a sense of vitality in the article?

d. Identify three anecdotes the writer uses.

e. Identify three effective quotations the writer uses. Explain why the quotations work well.

f. Identify three descriptions the writer uses to "show" instead of "tell."

g. Identify three literary devices the writer uses.

h. Write an essay of 300-400 words explaining why the article is effective.

✍ 14 ✍

Final Steps to Publication

WHAT YOU WILL LEARN IN THIS CHAPTER

• You must use the proper mechanical format for your article manuscript.

• Whether you submit your manuscript by regular mail or email, you must follow the appropriate procedures.

• After submitting your article to an editor, you will work with the editor at other stages with which he or she needs your help.

After you've put the finishing touches on your article, you must put it into the proper manuscript form and submit it to the magazine. Depending on the editor, you might be asked to help with details before publication, or you might not hear anything until the magazine publishes your article.

Preparing the Manuscript

Properly formatting your manuscript is a simple matter, and it is important that you use the correct form. Whether you mail a print copy of the manuscript to the editor or you email it, the format will be the same. Formatting simply involves placing the right information on the manuscript page and giving it a clean, professional look.

As you format your manuscript, here are the guidelines to follow:

1. Leave a margin of about 1 inch around all edges of the page.

2. At the top left of the first page, include your name, mailing address, and email address.

3. At the top right of the first page, indicate the number of words in your article. The count is important to give the editor an immediate indication of how long the article is.

4. Skip about one-half of the way down the page and then center the title of your article. The large space between your email address and the title allows room for the editor to make production notes.

5. Below the title, center your byline. The name may be the informal, normal one you go by, or it may be a variation of your name that you formally use with published articles.

6. Skip two spaces and begin typing the text of your article.

7. Double-space the lines in your manuscript.

8. Use 12-point type as the font size. [Note that the example on the following pages uses small type because of this book's page size.]

9. Use a readable font such as Times New Roman. (Make sure it is a normal looking font. Don't attempt to look "fancy.")

10. For the indention at the beginning of each paragraph, use a *tab*. Don't use automatic formatting for the indention.

11. If your article has numbered or bulleted lists, insert the numbers and bullets manually. Don't use automatic formatting. The reason is that most magazines use page design programs that don't import such automatic formatting.

12. At the bottom of the page, include the word "more" to indicate that the manuscript has additional pages.

13. After the first page and on subsequent pages, include a "folio line" at the top of the page. This folio line includes your last name, the title of your article, and the page number. At the bottom of each page, except the last one, include the word "more."

14. On the manuscript's final page, include the word "end."

The *Writing Advantage* feature "Manuscript Format" on pages 207-210 provides an example of the pages of a manuscript.

Before you submit your manuscript to the editor, you have one last opportunity to assure that it is clean and professional and that your article is well written. The *Writing Advantage* feature "Manuscript Analysis" on pages 212-213 provides a checklist of the most common mistakes writers make in putting together their first articles. It covers both formatting mechanics and the most important

Manuscript Format

Zack Smith
P.O. Box 22222
Tuscaloosa, AL 35401
zsmith@imawriter.com

Approx. 1,100 words

THE BIG CHRISTMAS TREE
by Q. Zachariah Smith

Where I grew up in Texas, it rarely snowed. The first snow I remember fell at Christmastime when I was 9 years old. It happened to be on the same day that my 12-year-old brother and I had planned to go out and find a Christmas tree and cut it down. We didn't know it would be one of the worst days of our lives.

Our father didn't like the idea. He didn't even like to decorate at Christmas. "The simpler the better" was his motto. He particularly didn't like big trees.

As soon as my brother and I had eaten breakfast, we were ready to set off. Daddy cautioned us, "Don't go too far, and if it starts to snow, come home immediately. And, no matter what you do, don't get a big tree. Get a small one that you can carry. No big trees!"

(more)

Smith / Big Christmas Tree / page 2

My brother and I had a different idea. We wanted the biggest tree we could find. There were acres and acres — miles and miles — of trees just across the pasture behind our house. We knew we could find the perfect tree. In our minds, that meant not only a tree shaped just right but a huge one.

There was no such tree at the edge of the woods. So we plunged in. We looked at one tree after another — but one would be too small, another not shaped like a perfect cone, another not covered thickly enough with needles. But we were convinced that within the next hundred yards or so we would discover the exact tree we were hunting.

Around 3:00 in the afternoon, it began to snow — slowly at first, and my brother and I barely noticed. By 4:00, though, the snowflakes were huge — the size of quarters — and the tree branches and dead winter grass and fallen leaves were hidden under a white blanket.

It was at about that time that we suddenly saw the tree we had been looking for. It must have been 12 feet tall. We were so impressed that it didn't even dawn on us that the tree was much too big to fit into our house.

We got out our hatchets and began hacking away. It was a hard job, and by the time we had finally got the tree cut down, the sun, hidden behind the snowy clouds, had almost set.

My brother and I grabbed hold of the tree trunk — and suddenly realized that, with our minds so focused on finding a tree, we had paid no attention to where we were going in search of it.

We set off in what we thought was the most likely direction home. But as the woods got darker, we realized we were lost. We went on for several hours, hoping we soon would figure out where we were. With each step, we were more exhausted and, we feared, more lost.

(more)

Smith / Big Christmas Tree / page 3

For the first two or three hours, we continued to drag that big tree behind us. With each step we took, it seemed to get bigger. It certainly got heavier.

But the last thing we wanted to do was give it up. It was like a treasure, as valuable, in our children's minds, as a chest of gold and jewels to pirates. We had searched for it so long, and it was the last thing we could think of losing.

Finally — barely able to carry it any farther and becoming more and more afraid that we could never find our way home and would freeze to death that night in the woods — my brother and I conferred.

We decided to drop the tree.

It was a hard decision, but the choice seemed to be between leaving the tree or freezing. That was around 9:00 o'clock. By then we were hungry (we hadn't eaten since early morning), tired and shivering.

We continued to walk, probably in circles, hoping that soon we would catch a glimpse of our home in the distance.

In the meantime, around 4:30, when the snowflakes were getting thick, our worried father had begun anxiously watching for us. As the sun was starting to set and light fade from the gray sky, he decided to set out to find us. Our mother had started praying.

Daddy walked for what must have been miles, but he returned to the house around midnight and told Mother he had seen no sign of us.

It was a short time after that that my brother and I, utterly lost and by now losing hope of ever getting home, suddenly saw a dim, small light flash on in the distance. It must have been at least a mile from us. It could be a barnyard light, we thought, or even, we wished, a light at our home. But if it came from our home, what could it be? The light was too high up to be shining from a window, and our house didn't have an outdoor light.

(more)

Whatever it was, though, it was a light of hope.

We began walking through the deep snow as quickly as we could. We forgot how exhausted we were.

We must have walked for an hour, but suddenly we found ourselves at the edge of our pasture. We crawled under the barbed-wire fence. There was the familiar barn in the distance. We began running: past the barn, past the garden — and then home!

Our father and mother saw us as soon as we ran into the yard. Mother grabbed us and quoted excitedly from her favorite song, "I once was lost, but now I'm found."

And then we saw what had made the strange light we had seen in the distance, high in the air.

Daddy had attached a 150-watt light bulb to the end of a long extension cord, climbed to the top of the big oak tree in our front yard, tied the bulb to the tip of the highest limb he could reach, 80 feet up, and turned on the light. Mother, in her joy at having my brother and me home, exclaimed that it "was like 'the light that lighted the world'!"

The next day, Daddy went out and bought 100 strings of Christmas lights and wrapped them all around that tree. People who lived in the area said for years afterward that it was the biggest Christmas tree they ever saw.

(end)

structure and style issues. Once you have the manuscript ready to go, you should go through the checklist to determine if it has any problems.

Submitting the Article

Once you are confident your article is ready, submit it to the publication either by regular postal mail or by email. Use the means that the editor prefers. Magazine entries in the *Writers Market* handbook and in a publication's writing guidelines will let you know what the editor prefers. If you cannot determine which one to use, simply email the editor and ask.

If you submit your article *by regular mail*, include a brief cover letter. It should not be elaborate. Address it professionally, and simply say something such as "Enclosed is my article ['Title of Article'] that you requested. Thank you for considering it. If I may provide any other information, please don't hesitate to let me know."

Along with the cover letter and manuscript, include a postcard, with a stamp on it, addressed to yourself. On the backside, type a message such as "[Name of magazine] has received your article ['Title of Article']." The postcard makes it easy for the editor to let you know your manuscript arrived. If you don't send a card, you may be left wondering if your manuscript ever reached the editor.

If you submit your article *by email*, in the subject line identify your message as a manuscript submission and its title — something like this: "Article you requested: 10 Tips for Budget Back-to-School Shopping." You want to be assured that the editor doesn't get your article confused with junk mail or spam. The subject line will identify your email as something the editor has requested.

Include a brief letter as the body of your email, just as you would if you had submitted the manuscript by regular postal mail. Indicate that you are attaching the article as a file. Then be sure that you actually do attach the manuscript file to your email. (There are occasions when an editor might not want you to attach the article to an email, but instead send it within the body of the email. Make sure you know which method the editor prefers.)

Working with Editors

After submitting your article to the editor who either requested it from your query letter or assigned it to you, you will work with the editor at other stages with which she needs your help.

This partnership with editors can vary from article to article and from mag-

Manuscript Analysis

Some problems frequently show up in manuscripts, especially when writers are trying to produce their first articles. Following is a list of some of the most common problems. Once you've completed your manuscript, double-check it against these points.

Problems with manuscript format

____ No headers or footers (page numbers, etc.)

____ Didn't space down far enough on the first page

____ No word count

____ No article title

____ No byline

Problems with mechanics: spelling, punctuation, editing

____ Carelessness/failure to edit

____ Commas

____ Spelling

____ Possessives

____ Word choice

Problems with slant

____ No specific slant

____ Too general for the magazine: Article could very well be published in a general-interest newspaper

---

azine to magazine. Many editors accept by submission and then only correspond with authors to say "thank you" and send them a check. Other editors ask for verification material on sources and other factual details that authors use. Still other editors have authors rewrite sentences and paragraphs.

Some editors will ask for no help in the editing stage, while some will have you do numerous rewrites. How much an editor asks of you will depend on the nature of your project and the personality of the editor.

In all situations, though, it's a reality that your editor will do at least some editing on your article. Editors will make changes — and it's their absolute right to do so. That's why they're called editors: They edit.

In working with editors, keep the following principles in mind:

_____ Lead is not slanted to the magazine's readership
_____ Too provincial — limited to a certain area
_____ Too academic for a magazine or newspaper

Problems with thematic unity
_____ No thematic focus
_____ Too much information in the first paragraph
_____ Conclusion does not connect with the rest of the article
_____ Point of view changes during the article
_____ Poor transitions

Problems with paragraph unity
_____ No thematic unity in paragraph — several ideas in same paragraph
_____ Divide longer paragraphs into shorter ones so that paragraphs don't include more than one idea

Problems with substance
_____ Article needs fuller development
_____ Sources of information need to be indicated
_____ Ideas need to be elaborated more fully, providing all details necessary for readers to clearly understand

Problems with vitality
_____ Use more anecdotes and examples
_____ Don't rely only on quotes
_____ Instead of paraphrasing what people said, use more direct quotes

---

• *Editors only want what's best for their publication.*

If the editor asks you to make changes, or if she alters your writing, it's because the piece needs to fit better with what the magazine needs. Editors know their publications inside-out and know how your article will best fit their pages.

• *Do your best to provide what the editor needs.*

If the editor needs extra help, try to accommodate him as much as possible.

• *Don't take editing personally.*

I'll not forget the time I received a contributor's copy of a magazine in the mail and turned the page to read the article I had written. I didn't recognize the first two paragraphs, the body of the article had been completely reorganized (and with a lot of wording changes), and all subheads had been rewritten. If my byline had not been on the article, I'm not sure I would have recognized it. Most freelancers have probably had a similar experience.

Instead of taking personally the changes in my article, I chalked it up to an eager editor and welcomed the paycheck I received — although I did think carefully about whether I wanted to propose other articles to the same editor.

• *Keep your communication professional.*

Do your best to cultivate good professional relationships with editors. Good relations are one of the best ways to assure that editors keep accepting your ideas and giving you article assignments. Be courteous. Be professional and polished. Provide top-notch articles on time. If you do, there's a good chance you'll keep seeing your name in print.

Now that we've gone through the complete process of feature writing, only one thing remains to be done. You need to take action. Come up with ideas, query editors, and start getting published!

Exercises

1. Take an article you have written for a magazine, and format it according to the guidelines explained in the section titled "Preparing the Manuscript" on pages 205-211 in this chapter.

2. After you have formatted the article in Exercise 1, check it against the points listed in the *Writing Advantage* feature "Manuscript Analysis" on pages 212-213.

3. Write a brief cover letter to accompany the article you chose in Exercise 1 in preparation to submit to an editor.

4. Determine whether the editor to whom you plan to submit the article prefers submissions by email or by regular mail. Then submit the article.

✒ 15 ✒
Business, Legal, and Ethical Practices for Writers

WHAT YOU WILL LEARN IN THIS CHAPTER

• Feature writers must pay attention to business, legal, and ethical issues.

• Writers must understand standard contracts and the rights they are selling to publications.

• Writers must set up a professional working environment and keep good records.

• Writers must understand copyright law, in order to be aware of their own copyright protection and to avoid copyright infringement.

Yes, feature writing is a creative endeavor — but the life of a professional writer is filled with procedures and challenges that are not necessarily creative. It requires organization and knowledge of business and legal requirements. Writers have to be diligent about matters such as selling their rights, signing contracts, maintaining an office, keeping records, honoring copyright, and filing taxes — things that may not appeal to the creative writer but that are necessary.

This chapter will cover the most essential business, legal, and ethical issues with which feature writers must deal.

Understanding Your Rights

When a feature writer sells an article to a publication, she also sells a particular type of right. The publication, in turn, is buying the rights to publish the article in any number of ways. It is claiming, for specified uses, ownership of the article.

Magazines, newspapers, and online publications have various guidelines for buying rights from authors — and some of them are better for the author than others. The types of rights they may buy from you include the following:

All Rights

The publication is buying all of your ownership to the article, and you are giving up the right to use it again. If possible, you should avoid selling all rights. Remember that, as mentioned earlier in this book, you should try to get as many publications as possible out of one article.

First Rights

The publication is purchasing the right to publish the article for the first time. After it has published your article, the rights to it belong to you again. This type of right is also sometimes called "first North American rights" or "first serial rights."

Reprint Rights

The publication is purchasing the right to republish an article that has already appeared previously in another publication.

One-time Rights

The publication is buying the right to publish your article only one time. This right is the most common type that magazines purchase, and it is the ideal arrangement for freelance writers. In fact, if a magazine does not spell out for you the rights it is buying, you should assure that it understands it is getting only one-time rights. In selling these rights, you have total control of your article after a magazine has published it once. You can sell it to other publications, making as much money as possible from it.

Electronic Rights

Many publications want to purchase the right to place your article on their websites along with publishing the article in print. Electronic rights give the publication permission to do so.

Multiple Submissions

It's difficult to get many articles published if you query on only one idea at a time. However, many publications ask that you not send them "multiple submissions." So, as a writer who desires publications and payment, what do you do?

In dealing with the dilemma, it's important first to understand the concept of multiple submissions. Sending multiple submissions means that you are sending the *same article to more than one magazine at the same time*. It would be an ethical issue if you had competing magazines (magazines that have the same audiences) with your same article on slate for publication. Ethical and intelligent ways exist, though, to increase your chances of success *and* not cause a problem among different publications. Here are the two basic principles to follow:

1. *Do send as many query letters on the same article idea to as many magazines as you can think of.*

While you must not send the same, complete article to competing magazines, you should send query letters to as many magazines as possible. All of them will not be interested in your idea, but perhaps one or more will be.

Imagine, though, that you have created a list of 10 magazines you think might like the idea and you send a query to only one magazine at a time, waiting to get a response from it before querying the next magazine on your list. Also imagine that, on average, it takes each magazine one month to reply to your query and that the first one to accept your idea is the seventh one you query. That means it would take seven months before you get a go-ahead.

Instead of waiting so long, go ahead at the beginning and send queries to all 10 magazines.

2. *Do not send the same manuscript to competing magazines, but come up with other slants to the same general idea.*

Most competing magazines — all women's magazines or all teen magazines, for example — publish articles on the same general topics (health, relationships, diet, etc.). Thus, several of them could be interested in the same idea about which you query. If you send out multiple queries at the same time, then, it is possible that more than one magazine will give you a go-ahead.

If more than one magazine wants your article, you then have the following options:

a. You could send your article to only one magazine and tell the others of your decision.

    b. You could send your article to one magazine — and not reply to the other magazines — and then, in the event the first magazine decides not to publish the article, send it to a second magazine.

    c. You could write an article for each of the magazines that give you a go-ahead, with each article taking a distinctive approach to the idea. Multiple articles on the same general idea are not a problem. Keep in mind that magazines in the same field publish numerous articles about the same topics issue after issue. If two or more magazines want an article from you, simply assure that you use different material — such as sources, quotations, and anecdotes — for each article.

    When you sell an article to one magazine, take your success as an indication that you have a good idea, one that might interest other magazines. So work with the idea, slant it differently, and propose an article to a competing magazine.

How (and How Much) Will You Get Paid?

One of the primary concerns for freelance writers is payment. As you start out in feature writing, it is useful to understand how you will get paid for your work. Magazines pay in either of the following two ways:

On Publication

    Some publications will pay a writer when an article appears in print or online. Depending on how far in advance a publication prepares its issues, the writer could wait months — perhaps as long as a year — to receive payment.

On Acceptance

    Other publications, including a majority of the larger ones, pay on acceptance. Once you've submitted your article and the editor accepts it, the magazine will send you the payment — even if it's months before the article is scheduled to come out in print or online.

    The amount writers get paid varies greatly from publication to publication. A publication's audience, circulation, and ad revenue play a big part in how much it pays writers. Smaller, niche magazines, have smaller budgets. Trade magazines, while very specialized, often pay as well as the larger consumer magazines.

    Magazines usually pay the following rates:

By the Word

A magazine may pay by the word. If, for example, a magazine pays 10 cents per word and you write a 1500-word article, you would receive $150. The amount that magazines pay can range from a few cents to a few dollars. A magazine that pays $1 per word is considered a high-end publication.

A Set Amount

Many magazines pay a set amount, which is agreed upon in the contract before the writer accepts an assignment or after the editor accepts an article based on a query letter from the author. The amount varies widely from publication to publication, ranging from $25 to more than $1,000. Most middle-tier magazines offer between $100 and $500 per article. Some magazines may pay several thousand dollars for an article — but in most cases, only writers with established reputations get such sums.

A Reprint Rate

If the writer sells an article that another magazine has already published, the second publication will pay a reprint rate. The reprint rate varies among publications, but it is usually under $50 or, among larger magazines, 10% of the original payment.

A Kill Fee

Magazines usually give a kill fee to the writer if it is unable to publish a planned article. The fee is typically 10% of the agreed-upon payment. If you've signed a contract for a $250 article, for example, you'd get $25 if the magazine does not publish it. Then you'd be free to publish it in another magazine.

Writers can learn more about payment rates and policies by reading the *Writer's Market* guide, by doing an Internet search with a term such as "how much do magazines pay for articles?" and by checking out an individual magazine's writing guidelines.

Understanding Your Publishing Contract

Once an editor assigns an article to you or agrees to publish an article based on a query letter from you, you will usually receive a contract or agreement. Although the words "contract" and "agreement" have different legal meanings, in practical terms they are virtually the same for freelance writers. For convenience, we'll simply use the word "contract" in this discussion.

Contracts are usually straightforward, with few areas for the publication to "cheat" the writer. It still helps, though, to know what you're looking at. Although the details are usually standard ones, if you question any point, you should not be hesitant to ask the publication to reconsider it. Ultimately, every detail is negotiable — although you should realize that, in nearly every instance, writers have little reason to want a change in the standard contract. A contract usually covers the following items.

1. *Rights Being Purchased*

Be sure to understand the information about rights as discussed earlier in this chapter. If you don't feel comfortable with the rights a magazine offers to buy, discuss the details with the editor and see if negotiation is possible. But weigh your desire to get published against your desire to limit the rights you're selling. If a major magazine wants to buy all rights, for example, it might be worth giving them up as a trade-off for building your portfolio.

2. *Arrangement for Payment*

The contract will spell out how much you are to be paid and whether you will be paid on acceptance or publication.

3. *Editing Arrangements*

Most contracts contain a standard sentence that reads something like "[The magazine name] reserves the right to edit for space and style." This clause can mean many things. The magazine may edit within limited parameters (meaning it won't alter your article drastically), it may let you see the changes before it begins the production process, or it may edit as completely as it sees fit and not let you be involved in any way.

4. *Word Count*

A contract based on a query you submit will give you a specific word count or at least a range for the length of the article. When you submit your manuscript, it must fall within the length the contract specifies.

5. *Content Details*

The contract will provide information about specific details that the editor wants you to use in your article. The details can include such things as points the article will stress, specific sources to be quoted, and writing tone.

6. *Specs for Subsidiary Items*

Did you tell the editor in your query letter that you would submit sidebars, photographs, or illustrations? If you did and the editor wants them, the contract will spell out the specifications for such items the editor expects you to provide.

7. *Arrangements for Author Copies*

The contract will tell you how many copies the magazine will give you of the issue in which your article appears.

8. *Due Date*

If you are working on assignment, the contract will give you a deadline for submission.

9. *Signatures*

The contract will have a space for both the editor's signature and your signature. Many magazines will also ask you to put your social security number next to your signature. It is used for reporting payment and income to the IRS.

The *Writing Advantage* feature "Standard Article Contract" on pages 222-223 provides an example of a typical agreement.

There may be times when you don't receive a contract or agreement. Some editors will simply notify you that the magazine will be publishing your article — along with details such as the word count, payment amount, and rights — and send you a check. As long as there is an understanding and it is in writing, this arrangement works well as an agreement between editors and writers.

Keeping an Office

Any business is more successful if it's run efficiently. One of the keys to business success for the feature writer is a well organized office.

To work efficiently, a feature writer needs a number of items, all of which can be housed in an office, a corner of an office, even a part of a bedroom. It is not necessary to have a writing-only office, but it is vital to have certain tools in whatever space the writer uses. Some of the most important items to have in your office or writing area are the following:

Desk
Computer with email and Internet access

Standard Article Contract

Agreement
.

1. Contract dated [insert date here] between [Name and address of publication] and [Name of Freelancer].

2. By signing this agreement below, the Writer acknowledges that [Publication name] has commissioned Writer to compose and write an article, story, script, or other written work (hereafter called "Work") about the subject.

[Here will be a description of the proposed/assigned article, including information about the content, tone, sources, etc.]

3. The Work shall consist of approximately [appropriate word count] words including sidebars.

4. The Work shall be submitted to [Publication name] via electronic submission as an attachment by email [or other appropriate instructions for submission].

5. The article manuscript shall be delivered no later than [due date]. [Publication name] may reserve the right to pay 10% less than the payment shown for each week it is late. If it is received too late for use, no payment will be made.

6. The Writer agrees that the completed Work will be considered a work made for hire

---

Recent edition of *Writers's Market* and other writing guides
Resource books (such as a dictionary, thesaurus, and grammar book)
Notebooks
File cabinet
Calendar
Log book or ledger
Camera
Tape or digital voice recorder

Keeping Good Records

Organization is an integral skill for a successful feature writer. It keeps you on

as defined in the prevailing copyright law. The Writer agrees that the Publisher is purchasing one-time rights to the Work [or other rights being bought by the publisher].

7. [Publication name] has the right to use the Writer's image, likeness, and biographical materials to promote the sale of the Work.

8. The Work must be in conformity with the guidelines and instructions given to the Writer. Writer will be paid a full and final payment in the amount of $ [amount].

9. Writer agrees that the Work has not infringed upon any copyright whatsoever.

10. This agreement shall be interpreted under the laws of the State of [name of state in which publisher is located] or applicable Federal laws.

11. This contract shall be effective upon the placing of signatures of both parties below.

_____ (Writer's signature)

_____ (Date)

_____ (Publisher)

_____ (Date)

Please sign and return one copy of this contract to:

Editor's name
Publisher's address

---

track and on schedule. You will know where you are on writing projects, and you can easily chart your progress. It's also important at tax time. If you begin making money at writing, you must pay taxes. Being organized will assure that you know how much income you have had and how much you can deduct for expenses — if you have the records to prove them.

Project Files

Writers need to keep all of the information for a particular project easily accessible. File folders — either in hard copy or on the computer — are the best way to keep information organized.

At the very least, set up a file folder for each individual article you're working on. In the folder, store clippings with information, notes you've written, different drafts, and other pertinent material on the topic.

It is also helpful to set up folders for ideas, information on subjects you might write about in the future, marketing, writing guidelines, and writing tips.

Project and Assignment Calendar

Keep track of projects on at least a desk calendar or page-a-day calendar. Write down your plans for each day, keep track of deadlines, and check off when you finish a project.

Query and Manuscript Submission Log

Use a notebook or computer document strictly as a query or manuscript log to record everything you send to magazines. Keep track of query letters by writing down the article idea, the magazine to which you send the query, and the date you send it. When you get a response from the magazine, log it. Do the same thing when you send out manuscripts. Write down the article title, the magazine to which you send it, and the response you get. On page 96 in Chapter 7 of this book, we included a standard form to use. You may wish to consult it as you create your own log.

Payment Log

A strong motivation for many writers is the compensation they get for their articles. Keeping a payment log is good for both motivation and business purposes. Keep track of your payments in a notebook or on the computer by writing down the article sold, the magazine to which you sold it, the amount you received, and the date you received it.

Keep a file of the payment checks you receive. Most checks come with a tear-away stub or a separate receipt of payment. If one doesn't, photocopy the check to use as a record.

Writing Expenses

For tax purposes, it's important to keep track of your writing expenses. If you're a working writer, you can deduct expenses. The IRS considers you a working writer if you make a profit three out of five years. Otherwise, it considers you a hobbyist.

Keep track of all expenses related to your writing. Retain receipts, canceled checks, and all other proofs that you spent money on any writing-related objects. Include such things as writing supplies, postage costs, photocopying, travel to writing-related destinations, books about writing, writing magazine subscriptions, writing conference fees, and writing equipment such as computers and printers. You can also claim a certain portion of your house if it is used solely for writing.

For convenience in filing income-tax statements, it is wise to keep a ledger that lists each expense, including the date and cost. On a separate page in the ledger, include each payment that you get for an article. Similarly, you might set up a ledger using a computer spreadsheet program such as Excel. Set up separate columns for different categories of items, such as income, mileage, office supplies, and postage. The spreadsheet will save you time when, as you're filling out your income tax returns, you must compute total expenses in different categories.

At income-tax time, calculating taxes based on income and expenses can be time-consuming. So you may find that a computer tax program such as TurboTax will be helpful and save you hours of work. To help offset its cost, you may deduct its price as an expense for your writing business.

The key related to expenses is to keep good records. If for some reason the IRS audits you, you must prove your deductions. So be certain to keep all of your receipts and use an organized system to file them.

Copyright

Feature writers need to understand copyright. It protects a writer's own work so that others may not steal or use it improperly. Writers also must be aware of copyright law so that they don't misuse other people's work.

The Copyright Act (Title 17 of the U.S. Code) protects original "works of authorship," which include most creative output — from literature, music, and paintings to movies, choreography, and computer programs. It protects the way an author or artist expresses an idea, principle, or fact — but it doesn't protect the underlying ideas or facts themselves. Copyright covers the following five key rights:

1. *Reproduction*: the right to create identical or substantially similar copies of the work

2. *Adaptation*: the right to create derivatives of the original work, such as abridgments, translations, and versions in other media — such as article to book and book to film

3. *Distribution*: the right to make the first sale of each copy of the work

4. *Performance*: the right to recite, play, dance, or act the work publicly

5. *Display*: the right to show the work publicly, directly, or by means of film, slide, TV image, or other device

Copyright protects a work for a very long time after its creation. How long depends to a large extent on when the work was created. The following provides a simplified explanation:

1. The easiest rule to understand is that if a work were created before 1923, its copyright protection has expired. That means that if you want to quote a novel, for example, published in 1922, you may do so without getting permission.

2. For works created between January 1, 1923, and December 31, 1977, copyright protection lasts for 95 years.

3. For works created on January 1, 1978, or later, the length of copyright protection depends on whether the work was an independent production or was "made for hire."

• An independent work is protected from the moment of creation and remains protected for the rest of the author's life and another 70 years after his death.

• If a work was made for hire — that is, for example, a piece written by an employee of a publication — copyright lasts 95 years after its first publication or 120 years after its first creation, whichever came first.

If you want more details about how long the copyright law protects works, you can find the information by doing an Internet search using a term such as "length of copyright protection."

Copyright Protection

Copyright law automatically covers your work when you put your ideas into tangible form. From the moment you express yourself on paper, on a computer, or online, copyright protects your expression. The protection will last until 70 years after you die.

Although copyright is automatic, authors can use the following two measures to strengthen their rights.

• The first is a proper notice: the word "Copyright" or the international symbol ©, the year of first publication, and the author's name or a recognizable abbreviation.

• Writers can also register a piece of writing with the federal copyright office. Although registration isn't required for a copyright to exist, it can be important if you ever sue someone for infringement. Information on registering your work can be found at the copyright office website: www.copyright. gov.

Once a magazine publishes an article, copyright covers the publication. Thus, the writer doesn't need to worry about registering the article.

Copyright infringement

Just as copyright protects a writer's work from being pirated, it also prohibits writers and publishers from improperly using material that they do not own. The Copyright Act makes it illegal to reproduce, adapt, distribute, or display other writers' work without permission. For the feature writer wanting to avoid violating the law, the key — put simply — is not to try to pass off another writer's work as your own.

The law does allow certain limited uses of copyrighted material. The "Fair Use Doctrine" provides that a writer may use some words from another for "criticism, comment, news reporting, teaching ..., scholarship [and] research."

The challenge comes, though, in knowing how much you may use in your own writing. There is no law that prescribes the exact number of words permissible. Whether one's use of another's words violates fair use depends on a variety of factors. Among the most important factors to consider are, in the words of the copyright law, "[1] the amount and substantiality of the portion used in relation to the copyrighted work as a whole and [2] the effect of the use upon the potential market for or value of the copyrighted work." That means, in essence, that the words a writer quotes must not make up a substantial part of either the original work or the new work, and the new work must not reduce the money-making potential for the original work.

For the feature writer who is not a legal expert, fair use is a matter of common sense. It's probably safe to use the "golden rule" in thinking about using someone else's words. If you'd be upset to find your work used the way you're using someone else's material, the use is probably unfair. When in doubt — especially if it's a large number of words being used — ask for permission to use the work.

As a matter of professional ethics, if you use someone's else's original idea or quote verbatim from a book, magazine article, website, or expert, be sure to name the source of your material. Tell readers that the information came from another source, and credit that source properly.

Sheree Martin
"Copyright and the Writer"

Q: What is the main purpose behind copyright law?

MARTIN: Copyright protection exists to promote the progress of science and the useful arts. The U.S. Constitution specifically includes copyright within the powers granted to the U.S. Congress.

Copyright law protects original works of authorship that are "fixed in a tangible medium," meaning the creative expression has been preserved through writing, musical or choreographic notation, painting, drawing, sculpture, audio/visual media, or other digital technology.

Q: Explain briefly what the difference is between facts and expression in the adage that you can't copyright facts but only the way the writer expresses them.

MARTIN: Facts exist without the need for creative expression. For example, this sentence is purely factual: John Wilkes Booth shot President Abraham Lincoln at Ford's Theatre on April 14, 1865. No matter how you arrange the words in this sentence, the expression is simply factual.

But if an author takes these facts and begins to expand upon them through research, analysis, and interpretation the author can develop an original work, such as a manuscript or painting, which is protected by copyright.

If certain writers were allowed to copyright facts, others would lose the building blocks needed for creative expression and the entire purpose of copyright protection would be defeated.

Q: If a writer wants to use words from the writings of another author, how much material can he use without getting permission from the original author?

MARTIN: A writer may only use the words from the writings of another author if the writer's use is a "fair use." There is no definite word count that qualifies as a fair use.

Taking an original phrase from a short poem or song might be an infringement, even if the phrase is only a few words.

On the other hand, using 75 words from a 300-page novel might be a fair use, depending on which 75 words the writer wants to use. It would not be a fair use, for example, to quote 75 words that are the essence of the plot dénouement.

In the case of a parody, though, it may be permissible to use the essence of the entire work, provided the writer isn't directly quoting the protected work.

Q: Since writing is automatically protected upon its creation, what is the advantage, if any, of registering it with the federal copyright office?

MARTIN: Registration establishes a record of authorship and ownership of copyrights. It can help a potential publisher find the copyright owner.

Registration is necessary to pursue a copyright infringement claim in federal courts under U.S. copyright law.

When a copyright is registered before an infringement occurs, the copyright owner will be eligible for statutory damages and can recover attorneys' fees from the infringer. Without registration before infringement, the copyright owner is limited to actual damages, which may be nominal if, for example, the infringement did not result in lost sales.

Q: What do you think the likelihood is that a magazine or other writer would steal a freelance writer's article or large chunks of it?

MARTIN: It's unlikely that a reputable magazine with a professionally trained editor will steal a freelance writer's article, but it's not unheard of.

It's more likely that a dishonest writer (or Internet "bot") will steal a writer's work. Thieves simply copy and paste the words they want to use. Software bots are set up to "scrape" websites and steal entire stories or pages for use on infringing sites.

Fortunately, it's much easier to find infringing uses today. For prolific writers who publish online, good blogging practices and relatively inexpensive security software exists to help bloggers minimize (or at least find) instances of scraping.

Q: What recourse, in practical terms, does a writer have if, for example, a magazine took his article and published it under the name of the editor?

MARTIN: Assuming the writer is the copyright owner, the writer should start by notifying the publisher and managing editor that the published work infringes the writer's copyright and demand that the infringer stop the infringement.

If the infringing use is published online, the writer should also identify the Web host for the site and submit a "takedown notice" under the Digital Millennium Copyright Act. The writer can use a "whois" search through a domain registrar to find the name of the ISP. A writer can find sample "takedown notice" letters at a variety of sites around the Web.

Filing a lawsuit for copyright infringement is also a possibility. ✍

Dr. Sheree Martin is a lawyer and assistant professor of visual and multimedia communication at Samford University, where she teaches a variety of courses, including media law. She is also a freelance writer and has a long list of published articles. She blogs at www.benfranklinfollies.com.

Libel

Along with copyright, writers also need to be aware of libel as a legal issue. Publishing libelous material can create serious problems.

What is libel? Simply put, it is anything *published* that is both *false* and *damaging*. It is similar to slander. Both involve defamation, but libel is printed defamation, and slander is spoken. To be libelous legally, printed information must be false, the writer must know that it is false or must have been very careless not to know it is false, and it must damage a person's reputation "in the eyes of a substantial and respectable minority" of readers (Restatement [2d] of Torts. § 559).

Generally, if you are ethical in your behavior, you won't have to worry about libel. What causes problems is careless disregard for facts and falsehood. Some writers make false statements simply because they don't double-check facts — not because they intended harm, but because they weren't conscientious.

Even if a problem does not escalate to libel, it's still important for a writer to practice professionalism and accuracy in the interviewing, sourcing, and writing process. As you research and write, keep these tips in mind:

1. Double check — actually, triple check — names.

Many people have similar names. As an illustration of this point, do an Internet search for a person's name. Unfortunately, newspapers and magazines regularly misspell names. To guard against such a mistake in your articles, always ask a source to spell his name for you, and then read it back to him for clarification. If a source has a common name such as John Smith, be sure to identify the individual in a way that specifies which John Smith he is. You might say, for example, "John Smith, who returned to his home town after serving as an artillery officer during the Persian Gulf War, died in a car wreck."

2. Check any facts about which you are not certain.

There are facts that you may casually assume are correct. If you have *any* facts mentioned in an article and you are not absolutely certain about them, verify them for accuracy.

3. Read material to your sources.

After an interview, read to the source any quotes that you anticipate using in your article. Make sure you are quoting him correctly. Do the same thing with any facts you want to check for accuracy. Ask the source if you're correct in what you wrote down.

Additional Questions?

A good resource for business, ethical, and legal questions is the Writers Union organization. Its website, www.nwu.org, provides information on any number of questions writers may have.

Exercises

1. If you haven't done so already, set up a home office or office area dedicated strictly for your writing.

2. Set up a file system on your computer, creating files for different topics and projects. Also set up an idea folder system.

3. Create a query log, manuscript submission log, and payment log.

4. Using *Writer's Market*, list five magazines that buy one-time rights and five others that buy all rights.

Magazines that buy one-time rights

    a.

    b.

    c.

    d.

    e.

Magazines that buy all rights

    a.

    b.

    c.

    d.

    e.

5. Select an article from a magazine or an online publication. Read the article, underlining any quoted material from other publications or individuals. How did the writer handle attribution of the quotes? How did he handle any permission to quote the material?

6. Write an essay of 300-400 words on the question: What are the most important ethical standards that a feature writer should live by?

Index